Rattlesnakes

Rattlesnakes

J. Frank Dobie

UNIVERSITY OF TEXAS PRESS, AUSTIN

INTERNATIONAL STANDARD BOOK NUMBER 0-292-77023-5
LIBRARY OF CONGRESS CATALOG CARD NUMBER 81-51879
COPYRIGHT © 1965 BY BERTHA DOBIE
ALL RIGHTS RESERVED
PRINTED IN THE UNITED STATES OF AMERICA

FOURTH UNIVERSITY OF TEXAS PRESS PRINTING, 1988
REPRINTED BY ARRANGEMENT WITH LITTLE, BROWN AND COMPANY, INC.

REQUESTS FOR PERMISSION TO REPRODUCE MATERIAL
FROM THIS WORK SHOULD BE SENT TO PERMISSIONS,
UNIVERSITY OF TEXAS PRESS, BOX 7819,
AUSTIN, TEXAS 78713-7819.

Contents

Rattlesnakes

Old Rattler, it is part of Nature's plan
   That I should grind you underneath my heel —
The age-old feud between the snake and man —
   As Adam felt in Eden, I should feel.

And yet, Old Rattlesnake, I honor you;
   You are a partner of the pioneer;
You claim your own, as you've a right to do —
   This was your Eden — I intruded here.

           —Vaida Stewart Montgomery
             "To a Rattlesnake"

Rattlesnake Lore

THE SCIENTIFIC FACTS about rattlesnakes are available in many places, ranging from the encyclopedia to the books of Raymond L. Ditmars, the great herpetologist. I have no objection to scientific facts; I expect to put down some of them; but I propose also to include yarns and gossip about rattlesnakes heard from people who never looked inside a scientific book. The rattlesnake in one form or another has been common to all of the United States; however, he grows larger in the West and Southwest, and somehow the talk about him in those regions seems bigger than elsewhere. Perhaps the sunshine accounts for this. Anyhow, over an enormous region of America talk about rattlesnakes is as common as talk about the weather, and this talk may be heard in law offices, hotel lobbies, and living rooms as well as around chuck wagons or on the friendly galleries of ranch houses.

Monsters

About the size of rattlesnakes: it is as difficult to determine the length of the biggest rattlesnake ever killed as it is to

[3]

determine the longest horn ever taken off a Texas steer or the biggest tusk ever extracted from a razorback boar. Yet measurements are not lacking.

There was the snake, for instance, that Rowdy Joe killed. One day back in the times before "barbed wire played hell with Texas," Rowdy was in the San Antonio stage with three other passengers. I shall let one of them tell what happened.

"We were rolling along at a pretty good pace when suddenly the two lead horses whirled and came back alongside the coach door and the stage came to a stop. The driver yelled out, 'Great guns, what a rattler!' There in the middle of the road was the largest rattlesnake I believe ever seen in Texas. It had struck at the leaders and apparently missed them, but had frightened them terribly. We all got out of the coach while the driver quieted the horses. Joe said, 'Just watch me cut that fellow's throat.' He had a Colt forty-five and stepped within about fifteen feet of the squirming monster, which was making a noise with his rattles that could be heard at least two hundred yards. Joe fired and, true to his word, he almost severed the head from the body at one shot.

"The driver declared that although he had lived in Texas all his life he had never seen such a rattler as this one. It was over eight feet long and as large around the body as the leg of a good-sized man. The rattles were twenty in number and about five inches long and as thick as my two fingers."

That was a monster snake, bigger than any ever seen in any zoo perhaps, and probably bigger than any ever seen by an accredited herpetologist. I have killed two rattlers over six feet long myself, and I can understand how one eight feet long would be regarded as a paragon. But bigger snakes — rattlesnakes we are talking about — have been killed. The Dallas *Weekly Herald* of July 28, 1877, reported a rattler killed in the Cherokee Nation, near Eufaula, eighteen feet long, with "thirty-seven distinct rattles on its tail." That report must have been exaggerated, but there is an old tradition that a rattler ten feet long with fifty rattles was killed by early settlers on the Colorado River of Texas.

Wes Burton, whom I have elsewhere tried to picture as a hunter of the lost San Saba Mine, told me this story. While he was putting down a shaft on Packsaddle Mountain he became acquainted with a farmer nearby named Jim Smith. Rattlesnakes were so numerous that they made cotton picking exceedingly dangerous for Smith's children. However, Smith had trained a dog named Booger to hunt out and bark at rattlesnakes. As the odor of rattlers, particularly of old ones, is very strong, it is not difficult for a dog to scent them at some distance. Old Booger stayed in the field all day with the children, scouting up and down the cotton rows ahead of them.

One morning, shortly after entering the cotton patch, the dog for some reason not being along, Smith's oldest girl came running to the house, crying to her father to come and kill the biggest snake it was possible to imagine. She had not seen him, but had come upon his "track," or drag, in the sandy soil. Smith called Booger and went at once. The snake's drag looked like that of a cotton sack, and Booger took it on the run. He was soon barking, but when Smith approached the snake and saw its size, he was afraid to attack it with the hoe he carried. So he went to the house for a shotgun, Booger continuing to raise Ned all the time he was gone. Having killed it, Smith got his wife's tapeline, which she used in sewing, and measured it. It was ten feet and four inches long. Wes Burton saw it shortly afterwards. He describes it as being of a variety known as "the red diamond, common in Arizona."

It may safely be said that in the Rio Grande Valley of Texas and in Northern Mexico rattlesnakes attain a larger size than they do anywhere else in the world. In the valley proper they are darker, more sluggish, and less vicious than they are out in the sands. W. S. ("Snake") King of Brownsville, Texas, who is credited with having handled more rattlesnakes than any other man in the world, claims to have captured alive, in Mexico, a rattler nine feet, six and one-half inches long. About 1914 Domingo Roach was running a steer in the lower Rio Grande Valley. Suddenly the steer went down to his brisket in a ratonera — a rat's den. When Domingo caught up he saw two gigantic rattlesnakes with their fangs fastened into the steer's jaws on either side. The steer bawled once and died. Domingo shot the rattlesnakes with a Winchester he carried on his saddle. The skin of one of these snakes, after it had been taken off and dried, measured ten feet and three inches from the tip of its nose to the last button of its rattle; the other skin measured nine feet and eight inches. For several years the skins were displayed in a drugstore at Harlingen. Captain Frank Hamer of the Texas Rangers had a rattlesnake skin, taken from the same region, nine feet eight inches long and sixteen and one-half inches across at its widest spread. In the express car that used to run on the Saint Louis and Brownsville Railroad into Brownsville was a stuffed rattlesnake said to be between fourteen and fifteen feet long. A snake's skin will stretch, but probably not more than an inch and a half to the foot.

Edward T. Soph, of Houston, has sent me what I suspect is a well-traveled anecdote of another big 'un.

One evening about dusk a farmer walked into his kitchen and told his wife he had just killed the biggest rattler he'd ever seen.

"Did you cut off the rattles?" she asked.

"No, I'll get them after supper."

After eating, the farmer walked out in pitch darkness, went to the spot where he'd left the dead snake, heard the slight quivering of the rattles, got hold of some of them and hacked off with his knife what he supposed was the entire string. Back in the kitchen, he and his wife counted eighteen rattles.

The next morning he went to carry the dead snake off and found that it still had enough rattles to make a noise.

The biggest rattlesnakes known are of the Eastern diamondback species. The largest one officially measured reached a length of eight feet or so. Next in size is the Western diamondback, with an official measurement of seven feet or so. But lots of snakes have been killed when no herpetologist was around to make measurements. The way to make a record in snake-killing is to be off away from tape measures or yardsticks or scales and not to have too many witnesses. One way to ruin a good story is to be overcautious on facts. I'm as eager after good stories as present-day fanatics in patriotism and posers in religiosity are to anoint themselves with the oil of self-righteousness.

The Abbé Domenech came to Texas in 1846 and wrote a book in French, an English translation of which was published in London in 1858 under the title of *Missionary Adventures in Texas and Mexico: A Personal Narrative*. This sprightly and often humorous account of marvels in man and other forms of nature on the frontiers is especially rich on rattlesnakes. Near Quihi, now in Medina County, the Abbé relates, "a tiger hunter killed a rattlesnake he had mistaken for a dead tree" fallen to the ground. (The hunter, I understand, had sat down on it to rest.) "The reptile measured seventeen feet in length, eighteen inches in circumference and had twenty-five rings, or rattles."

Of course it is human nature to exaggerate; we all like marvels to take us out of the normal routine. That is why the world is always in quest of heroes. But I for one am ready to believe that pioneers, coming upon a fresh rattlesnake world in which the reptiles had been very little molested, found an occasional one far beyond the average in length, just as giant men have been exhibited. The Karankawa Indians believed that a rattlesnake would never die of old age but would live indefinitely unless killed. Certainly snakes, like eagles, live when undisturbed by man to be very, very old, though America has become so "settled up" that the chances of any modern rattler to live a hundred years and become eighteen — or even ten — feet long are exceedingly few. The great handicap suffered by modern scientific naturalists is that nowadays they can observe among many animals only the escaped few instead of the unmolested millions; again, the man who has lived out a long lifetime has had chances to see rarities of nature that even the most active field naturalist, who necessarily spends a great deal of his time in classifying and recording and in reading books, is likely to miss. In short, some of the frontiersmen saw things in nature that no naturalist can now observe and that the majority of them will not credit.

The age of a rattler can no more be determined by the number of rattles it wears than a buck's age can be determined by the number of tines on his antlers. In crawling, a rattlesnake keeps his tail somewhat elevated, but even then the rattles of a big snake break and wear off. Add this to the fact that "buttons" are not added annually — like the rings on a tree — but one each time the snake sheds its skin, and it may be seen how impossible it is to rely on the number of rattles to determine the age of a snake. Many very large and old rattlers have almost no rattles. Incidentally, there is a trick of stringing two or three sets of rattles together on a thread and drawing them together tightly so that they appear to be off one snake; tenderfeet have paid good money for such apparently phenomenal sets of rattles.

Concerning the many legendary monsters that belong to the rattlesnake world of America, one tale must be representative. The inhabitants of the Arbuckle Mountains of southern Oklahoma have since the days of the first white settlers in that region believed that their rough land harbors "the king of all rattlesnakes." He is as broad as the back of a dog and as long as two ponies; his string of rattles is the length of a man's arm. In his head is a great diamond, and studding his long sides are other diamonds, so brilliant that they would dazzle the eyes of any man who gazed upon them in the light of the sun. Long ago, so the legend runs, a tribe of Indians brought this king of the rattlers into the Arbuckle Mountains to observe with him their customary religious ceremonies. To them the snake was sacred. But one time while they were in the midst of ceremonies they were attacked by hostile forces, and in their confused retreat they left the snake behind. He crawled off; he is still alive; and there are still men who hope someday to capture or kill him. His fangs have poisoned numberless cattle and horses; he has devoured calves. At various times in various places his track, as wide and deep as that of a buck deer dragged by a panther, has been seen. Once a hunter saw his awe-inspiring tail disappear into an inaccessible crevice called Rattlesnake Cave; again, his discarded skin has been found, the breaks and indentations in it showing that the king of the rattlesnakes still wears the wonderful jewels in his body.

Rattlesnake Dens

The largest number of rattlesnakes that have been found together in one place seems as unprovable as the size of the largest rattlesnake killed. Reports of dens that upon being dynamited have yielded from twenty to fifty rattlers are not uncommon. I have heard that in Oregon a single den yielded between six and seven thousand and that in Colorado another den gave up two thousand. Quién sabe? It is reliably stated that ninety-eight rattlesnakes were taken from a den near Coleman, Texas, in January, 1923. Certainly rattlesnakes have regular winter quarters to which they must gather from far distances, dispersing each spring with the coming of warm days. It is not likely that any den dynamited in the future, unless down in Mexico, will contain as many rattlesnakes as some dens already dynamited. For rattlesnakes are becoming fewer and fewer.

It would be contrary to the weavings of human imagination if these gathering places of rattlesnakes had not given rise to some extraordinary tales. In the Cheyenne and Arapahoe country of western Oklahoma is a famed hill called Cedar Mound. Pertaining to that hill is a legend, descended from some of the Plains Indians, that I have heard more than one white man tell.

Cedar Mound rises several hundred feet above the surrounding plain. To the west of it are other hills, but eastward the prairie stretches as far as the eye can reach. The top of the mound is a flat table carpeted with luxuriant buffalo grass and set with hundreds of cedar trees.

It is a good country for snakes, but snakes about Cedar Mound are only moderately numerous until the night of the first full moon in October, by which time northers and cool nights have heralded winter. Then, every year, they swarm up the sides of the hill and gather on top of the mesa by the thousands. At least, this is what legend says. Legend has an explanation.

Back in the days of the "sooners," before Oklahoma had been opened to homesteaders, several families had worked their way down from Kansas and were living at truce with the Cheyennes and Arapahoes. Then a great pestilence struck the whites. It must have been yellow fever. Within a short time the little colony was wiped out. Only one of the number was left — the buxom and comely wife of the leader of the band.

Alone in a world of coyotes, jackrabbits, and dead kinsmen, she had but one recourse. She took it. She threw herself on the mercies of the Cheyennes.

The "fighting Cheyennes," as they have been called, do not until this day have much use for the palefaces. In the time that this legend harks to, they were sullen from defeat in battle and their restriction to a cramped reservation. As a tribe, they spurned the white woman. But among them was a brave who looked upon her with favor. He took her into his tepee. Immediately the tribe disclaimed him and he was forced to leave.

Then, with his "white squaw," his weapons, and his tepee, he climbed to the isolated heights of Cedar Mound. The curses and evil prophecies of the medicine men of his tribe followed. And it was not long until those evil prophecies were fulfilled. The deadly plague that had carried off the other whites seized on the woman. At midnight before the first full moon in October she died.

The Indian brave was ashamed of the evil that had come upon him and he wished to hide it from the medicine men. So in the early dawn he took the body of the dead woman down the side of the hill and buried it in a cave, according to the custom of the woman's people.

The day passed, and then the next night a terrible thunderstorm came up. All the lightnings of heaven seemed to be dancing and shooting around Cedar Mound. Boulders were shaken loose from their moorings of centuries, and they tore down the hillside. The ceiling of the burial cave fell in, crushed some of the rattlesnakes that made it their den, and aroused all the others.

There were thousands of them, some of them great six-footers that had lived undisturbed in the cave for generations. All were enraged. Their rattling could be heard above the thunder. Rattlesnakes are wise, though, beyond all other serpents. They knew what had brought the disaster upon them. They moved to get vengeance.

The other rattlesnakes of the hills and prairies heard the rattling of those that had been run out of their cave, and now they joined in crawling to the top of the mound, where in his tepee shivered the once brave Indian who had brought on the storm's curse. There they found him, and there they wrapped their bodies about him and darted their poison into him.

Instead of dying at once, however, the Red Man went into a delirium and raced over the bodies of the snakes to a boulder that stood on the western edge of the mound. Only for a moment did he stand there. Then he plunged into the gulf below. The great boulder went with him, and together they crashed the hundreds of feet downward.

The boulder can still be seen at the foot of the bluff. The cave, littered with debris from its torn ceiling, can still be seen — if one wishes to run the risk of snakebite in exploring it. And to this day, on the night of the first full moon of each October, the rattlesnakes swarm to the heights of Cedar Mound. They come there to remind men of the curse pronounced against all Indians who marry into the white race. They come to remind men of the terrible fulfillment of the curse. And no man of that country who knows rattlesnakes would risk his life on that hill this one night of the year.

Joseph J. Good, who experienced much and whose memory was precise, told me that more than fifty years ago the Cross C Ranch where he was working had a noted den of rattlesnakes that he never saw but heard much talk about. Other cowboys told him that they had looked into a cave where rattlesnakes denned and seen a ball of them maybe four feet in diameter, the snakes all interlaced with each other, writhing like maggots. Sug Robinson, a noted cowman, told him that one time along in the 1880's while he was driving in a buggy through the country, the rattlesnakes got so numerous he whipped his team into a run in order to avoid having a horse bitten and being left afoot twenty miles from any house. Sug Robinson said that rattlesnakes would strike at the buggy wheels and get their heads caught between the spokes and that the flying wheels would hurl them over the dashboard right and left.

In the country between the Nueces River and the Rio Grande, rattlesnakes were once incredibly numerous. Down in the brush country along the Nueces River, I myself while out horseback most of one summer averaged killing three a day over a period of several weeks; but I know that before my time they were much thicker.

A chronicler of early-day Texas furnishes this account. In 1839 Cordova led a band of raiders into Texas from Mexico. The frontiersmen who gave him chase turned back at what was called the Prickly Pear Prairie, near the Nueces River — "a perfect den for rattlesnakes." From the time the Texans commenced traversing the pear flat until they were clear of it, "they were not out of the sound of rattlesnakes, and they had to pick their way carefully to avoid being bitten, as many of the horses had given out and the men were afoot leading them. . . . They gave up the pursuit here on account of the jaded horses."

Some Mexicans who had been with Cordova and were captured in a fight shortly afterwards said that if the Texans had followed them a little farther, they would have overtaken them, since Cordova stopped on the Nueces to bury a number of his followers "who had died from rattlesnake bites received during their passage through the pears."

On another occasion while some frontiersmen were scouting for water near Prickly Pear Prairie, they saw a bunch of mustangs dash out from a motte of brush. Thinking that the mustangs had probably been watering, they made for the brush to investigate; upon approaching it, they were met by a terrible stench accompanied by the warning notes of a rattlesnake. The mustangs had run over him, arousing him to anger, at which time rattlers exude the strongest odor. The snake, which was shot in the head with a rifle, measured "about nine feet long and was as big around as the thigh of a common-sized man."

Terribly Poisonous

Everybody has heard the story of the wagon tongue bitten by a rattlesnake. Presently it began to swell, and in order to save his wagon the freighter who owned it hurriedly chopped the tongue off with an axe. This happened a long time ago. By the obverse, it reminds me of a dispatch that came from Georgia in 1927.

Some workmen building a power line through a swamp aroused a rattlesnake, which in striking somehow hung his fangs in the tire of an automobile. The tire must have been very thin, for the fangs penetrated far enough to puncture the inner tube. They could not be withdrawn, and presently it was noticed that as the tire went down the rattlesnake was blowing up. "The air pressure was presumably transmitted through the hollow fangs of the reptile." Anyway, the reptile soon became so full of air that he exploded.

I want to tell something about rattlesnake poison that fell within my own experience. One summer while I was buying up a few steer yearlings near the Mexican border, I came to a small ranch, two or three sections of land, that had recently been acquired and improved by an old German who was laboring under the delusion that he could farm in that drouthy country. Yes, he had some "three-year-old yearlings" that he wanted to sell. If I would walk with him back to the watering trough in his pens, we could see them. I noticed that he had a good well and windmill at the pens and another good well and mill just across the road in front of his house.

After we had inspected the "three-year-old yearlings"

and were passing through his yard, I observed a fig tree that was dying. Fig bushes of any kind in that neck of the woods are about as scarce as hen's teeth.

"My goodness alive," I said, "you ought to be ashamed of yourself for letting a fine fig like that die for the want of water when you have so much of it."

"Huh," the old German replied, arresting his waddle and looking me straight in the eye. "You tink dat fig tree die for vater, you are fool."

"Well, what did it die of?"

"I tell you." And this was his story.

Two days before while passing near the fig he heard the angry warning of a rattler. He looked. At the root of the fig was coiled the biggest diamondback he had ever seen. He ran for a hoe, but upon raising it to chop the snake he considered that he might injure the bush, and so he decided to punch the snake away from it. The first jab or two of the hoe handle did nothing more than arouse the rattler to frantic anger. He struck at the handle, missed it, and sank his fangs in the tree. Immediately almost, by the time the snake was killed, the leaves on the fig began to wither.

"You see it now," the German concluded.

I saw it. It was certainly "plenty dead." I have heard that an extra-fine flavor can be imparted to a watermelon by running one end of a hollow straw through the cork of a brandy bottle, inserting the other end into the melon stem, and leaving the bottle to drain. A college professor who used to run a plantation in Mississippi told me that he once kept his best watermelons from being stolen by plugging some of them and inserting ipecac. In other words, it appears that the sap or juice of plant life can be inoculated. Still, although Mexicans have told me of seeing trees killed by the *sting* of a king snake, this fig tree is the only specimen of the vegetable kingdom that I have ever actually seen killed by rattlesnake poison.

How much poison does it take to kill? How long will the poison on the tip of a fang remain effective? The folk answer to these questions has often been expressed in a tale that takes on many forms. Here is one form.

A cowman in Oregon by the name of Garley had a buxom young wife and a very handsome pair of shopmade boots. One day while he was out in his new boots, a rattlesnake bit him on the foot through the leather. He barely had time to reach home and tell his wife that he had been snakebitten before he expired. His wife took possession of the ranch and boots and within a few months she had an admired friend named Swanton in charge of her business. He liked to spend his nights about headquarters. One morning when Swanton sallied forth he was wearing Garley's boots. By night he was near death. He died. A little blister was found on his foot. The boot he had worn was examined. A rattlesnake fang was still in it. People said, "Just retribution."

One form of this folktale supposes a cowboy who was going courting in a new pair of boots to have been bitten. He dies, leaving the boots to a dear friend. The friend will not for a long time profane the gift by using it, but he falls in love with the lovely girl that his friend was courting, and pulls on the beautiful boots in order to appear well before her. He sickens and dies, leaving the boots to a friend of his. They are very fine boots, embroidered and silvered. This third cowboy, in time, falls in love with the still unwedded girl and "dolls up" in the boots to court her. He sickens and dies. People begin to suspect the girl of exerting some fatal influence; then it is discovered that there is a rattlesnake fang in one of the boots.

Another common story runs this way. While a fence-rider was one day picking up the end of a broken wire to splice it, he was without warning bitten on the thumb by a rattlesnake. He had a sharp hatchet in the other hand; at once he laid his thumb, already turning black, against a post and chopped it off. He wrapped his hand up, padding it well with some cobwebs that happened to be on a bush nearby, so as to stop bleeding, and then shot the rattler. The wound healed so well that he did not have to stop work.

Not many days later the cowboy came again to the place where he had chopped his thumb off. He halted and saw it on the ground. While he no longer wore a bandage, the stub of his thumb was still rather raw. Idly, and perhaps with a good deal of sentiment, he now picked up the severed member of his own anatomy and began experimenting to see if it would fit against the stub. The virus in the thumb infected the hand, and he died of rattlesnake poison before he could reach a doctor.

How many severed rattlesnake heads have been fatal it would be impossible to estimate. Anyway the rattlesnake is so poisonous, and fear of his poison was so great among even the boldest of bad men in the Old West, that one successful California miner about to ship his "dust" on a stage subject to "road agents" placed three rattlesnakes in the trunk with his gold. It was not molested.

A good deal has been written about the use of rattlesnake poison on Indian arrowheads and lances, but, so far as I know, no scientist has gone to the trouble to follow the process commonly prescribed for getting the poison and then testing the effectiveness of weapons freshly treated with it. W. J. McGee in his notable work *The Seri Indians* describes how these people place rattlesnake heads, scorpion tails, and centipede feet with a putrefying mass of liver that has received rattlesnake poison until the mixture is gruesome beyond the conception of medieval witchcraft. While an arrow freshly treated from this "wizard's brew" might, he thinks, easily develop "morbific germs and ptomaines" that would "initiate septicemia" into a wound, yet the whole business is "on the plane of shamanism and sorcery."

Doubtless there is a good deal in McGee's argument. The Digger Indians are reported to have rendered their shafts deadly by a combination of rattlesnake poison with an extract distilled from some plant known only to themselves. "This plant would appear to possess the qualities of the fabled upas tree, as the noisome vapors exhaled by distillation act so powerfully upon the procurer as to destroy life. It becomes therefore a matter of some moment to decide upon the individual who is to prepare the yearly stock of poison for the tribe. Now it would naturally be supposed that so dangerous an office would be shunned by all; on the contrary, a yearly contest takes place among the oldest squaws as to which shall receive the distinguished honor of sacrificing her life in the cause, and the conflict ends in the appointment of the successful competitor, who does the work and pays the penalty."

Despite the "wizard's brew" and the story of the fatal plant, preparing poison for weapons was with many North American Indians — and with some of them still is — a quite simple business altogether devoid of magical significance. The most widely experienced and the most interesting hombre del campo I was ever out with was C. B. Ruggles. It goes without saying that he had an inquiring mind, a lively imagination, and an extraordinarily observant eye. My chief association with him was on a muleback trip across the Sierra Madre. He hunted and prospected pretty much up and down the North American continent from the most remote parts of Alaska to Durango. I shall have occasion later on to quote him respecting the Hopi snake dance. What he told me concerning the preparation and use of rattlesnake poison by Indians coincides with what other outdoor men have testified.

One time — this was in the early 1920's — while prospecting in the Pima Indian territory of the Sierra Madre, Ruggles left his animals in camp and was following afoot down a canyon when he noticed that some leaves had been freshly cut from a maguey plant growing alongside the trail. Of all the agaves of Mexico and the Southwest the maguey probably grows the strongest and hardest dagger tip on its leaves. Ruggles saw the tracks of two men ahead of him in the trail; then he saw where the tracks pulled out. Just beyond this point he noted some coarse-stemmed sacatón grass bent over the trail to make the passage narrower. Instinct told him to be cautious. Half concealed by the bent grass, the imprint of a man's knuckles showed in the soil. Those knuckles had been tamping a maguey leaf into the side of the trail so that the dagger point would prick the foot or ankle of unwary pedestrians. Other tips were concealed in a similar manner. Ruggles examined them. They all bore a kind of powder that Ruggles knew to be poison.

In time he learned how the Pimas prepare poison for weapons. The process they use has been used by Indians all over Western America.

The Indian first ties a thong into the edge of a deer's liver, so that he can swing it; sometimes he fastens it to the end of a stick. Liver dries quickly on the outside and holds its blood in liquid form for a long while. Taking the liver with him, the Indian goes in search of a rattlesnake. He does not have to go far. When he finds the snake, he swings the liver, at the end of the thong, in front of the snake's head. The snake strikes and leaves his venom in the liver. The Indian torments his "friend" — for so he regards the rattlesnake — until all its poison has been extracted. He repeats the process on rattler after rattler, filling the liver with venom from ten or twelve snakes.

Then he places the poisoned liver in an olla, or earthen jar, stretching over the mouth of it a piece of buckskin so perforated as to keep out insects and yet allow air to enter. He places the olla among sunbaked rocks but never directly in the sun's rays. In a little time the liver swells up so as nearly to fill the olla. It has the look of green foam. After some days it dries to the brittle lightness of a cow chip. The dried substance is then taken out of the olla and placed on a hard, clean rock, where it is ground with a stone into a fine, fine powder.

The preparation of the poison is now complete, but the powder must be carefully preserved. To receive it, the Indian takes the floater, or air bladder, of a fish, cuts it into a kind of pocket, cures it, and perhaps oils it on the outside so as to add to its waterproof nature. This pocket is put inside a buckskin sack of double thickness, which has a puckering string that can be tied and then looped around a man's neck.

Thus the Indian carries his poison. The perspiration of

years may soak through the buckskin, but it will not soak through the fish bladder and thus form a solution to ooze out on the man's skin. If the Indian wants to poison a dagger from the maguey or any other sharp point, he merely opens the little bag suspended from his neck, dampens the point to be poisoned, and inserts it into the sachet. Sometimes he dips the edge of a knife into the powder also. Once the poison gets into the blood of a victim, blood poisoning is almost certain.

Cures for Rattlesnake Bite

Captain Frederick Marryat has, in his wild hit-and-miss *Narrative of the Travels and Adventures of Monsieur Violet in California, Sonora, and Western Texas,* a marvelous story about how the hero was bitten by a rattlesnake and had resigned himself to death when he "beheld five or six stems of the rattlesnake weed." He had often heard of this weed from the Indians. Fortunately he had a vessel of water boiling on his campfire; he at once made a strong tea of the roots, which he drank and applied to the wound. Needless to say, he was absolutely cured of the bite.

All my life I have heard of the rattlesnake master weed, snakeroot, snakeweed, or hierba de víbora, as it is variously called. For many years I have been trying to find out just what it is. A "yarb-woman" from Arkansas who once worked for us contributed the information that in her state a certain wild hyacinth is so well known as a master weed that if one rattlesnake is bitten by another it at once seeks this plant, eats some of it, and recovers. According to Negroes of the Louisiana swamps, what they call "Samson-snakeroot," a member of the pea family, is so efficacious that it will not only cure rattlesnake bites but, if a bit of it is carried in the pocket, will prevent a snake from biting one. In Oklahoma the squatters on Indian lands relied upon the niggerhead, or purple-rayed cone-flower (a member of the *Brauneria* group), to master the rattlesnake bite. When we come to the snakeweeds and roots listed by the botanists, we are dumbfounded at their number and variety. Each locality has had its master weed — probably all of them equally masterful. In general, however, the aboriginal herbalists of the rattlesnake's habitat seem to have regarded with most favor some variety of milkweed, or, at least, a weed giving forth a milky juice.

Regarding the Texas milkweed, known also as rattlesnake milkweed (*Asclepias texana*), a representative story has come down. An Indian chief with five of his warriors once called at a ranch home in the hill country above San Antonio to ask for food. While they were eating, a member of the family rushed in announcing that a man had been bitten by a rattlesnake and was apparently dying. The Indian chief, upon learning the cause of the excitement, made a few motions to his men and they hurriedly scattered in various directions. In a short time one of them returned with roots of the Texas milkweed. These were mashed, some of the pulp applied to the wound, and some of it given to the patient internally. "The man became well in an unreasonably short time."

Yet the hierba de víbora which Mexican troops stationed along the Rio Grande used to carry in their pockets was of the acanthus family. The Mexicans were so confident of its antidotal powers that, according to a traveler through Mexico, several of them offered to submit themselves to a rattlesnake provided he would pay a dollar a bite and allow the victim to employ hierba de víbora on the wound immediately.

A very common remedy employed by Indians and pioneers was the Spanish dagger. Thousands of people still believe in its worth. The dagger points of this widespread variety of yucca are to be jabbed into the flesh all about the wound. The jabs cause bleeding.

The favorite folk remedy, however, has been whiskey — pure old bald-face, white mule, red eye, prickly pear juice, forty-rod liquor. Even today in the ranch and farm homes of many teetotalers a mellowing bottle of whiskey, tightly corked, awaits the dreaded rattlesnake bite. Doctors may declare that whiskey is the worst thing the victim of snake venom can take, for by increasing heart action the alcohol quickly disperses the poison over the system, but not many hunting parties will go forth without being well provided with "rattlesnake remedy." Whiskey is as good for rattlesnake bites as it is for colds.

At one of the frontier forts of western Texas occupied

by United States troops soon after the close of the Civil War, a soldier cutting weeds along the edge of a creek near his company quarters was one morning bitten by a rattlesnake. The captain took the case in hand and poured whiskey down the patient until he forgot all about being snakebitten. *Similia similibus curantur.* Shortly after this occurrence the company was ordered to "fall in" for inspection, and the roll was called. Paddy Maloney was reported absent. While the inspection proceeded, the captain chanced to look towards the creek. There he saw the absent Maloney, barefooted, his trousers rolled up to his knees, thrashing back and forth among the weeds. A corporal was dispatched to bring in the culprit.

"Private Maloney," demanded the captain in his severest tones, "what were you doing in those weeds and why were you absent from inspection?"

"Sor," replied the Irish soldier, "I saw the tratement John Burns got for his snakebite and, faith, I thought it worth me while to get a bite meself."

The captain ordered a quart of whiskey for Paddy with directions that it be drunk immediately.

But if there were no whiskey, if the Spanish dagger remedy seemed too severe, and if no snakeweed could be found — and comparatively few English-speaking homesteaders of America ever learned the weed well enough to rely on it — there were other remedies. One of the "reliable" cures for snakebite has always been to apply against the wound a freshly killed animal: chicken, rabbit, pig, crow, hawk, frog, nearly anything. The liver is really more effective for drawing the poison out than anything else, but just cut a chicken open while it is still fluttering with a broken neck and apply to the wound.

"One evening after dark while Father was puttering around in the cow lot, he was bitten by a rattlesnake," said a century-old woman who came to Texas in 1845. "We had to doctor him without a light. Mother had heard that warm flesh on the wound would draw out poison. She had a hen with a brood of chickens under the floor of our cabin, and every so often through the night she would reach down through a crack, get a little chicken, pull its head off, tear its body open, and apply it to the wound. When daylight came we gathered cockleburs, boiled them in sweet milk, and had Father drink the brew. Then we poulticed the wound alternately with cocklebur mash and dead chickens. He got all right."

If one could be so fortunate as to kill the snake that bit him and apply either the snake's liver or other parts of its flesh to the wound, the effect would be even better.

An old-time sheriff of West Texas contributes this remedio. One of two men out in a camp miles from anywhere was bitten on the hand by a large rattler. The other man quickly shot down a cow that happened to be standing close by, slit a hole in her belly, and had the wounded man thrust his arm inside up to the shoulder. The sun was broiling hot, so saddle blankets were propped up over the sufferer to make a shade. Late in the evening when the cow's body got cold he withdrew his arm. "It looked like a washerwoman's arm after a hard day's work, but the poison had all gone out of it."

Poultices were made of prickly pear, cow manure, garlic, onions and kerosene, tobacco leaves moistened in vinegar, clay and soot, grease and soot, mud, and so on.

Modern science has come to the conclusion that the best thing to do for a snakebite, pending the injection of antivenin, is to tourniquet the wound, then scarify, and suck the venom out — with some cupping device if possible; otherwise with the mouth. The tough old-timers sometimes followed this method; often they merely scarified the wound and then burned gunpowder, rosin, or some other inflammable *in the wound*.

One of the homemade remedies that the medical profession recognizes as being effective is to scarify the wound and put salt in it. The salt sets up the process of osmosis, thus draining off the poison. Scarification, salt, and proper tourniqueting will probably prevent death from any snakebite on the limbs of a body. Another folk remedy is to place the limb bitten — whether of man or beast — in a vessel containing kerosene and salt.

Potassium permanganate, long recommended by doctors and prescribed by the U. S. Army, is now regarded as being as worthless as rattlesnake weed or whiskey. And even the much touted antivenin has its questioners.

It may be laid down as a law of homemade medicine

that anything extraordinarily bad is extraordinarily good for something. Hence in popular lore "the finest remedy for rheumatism in the world is rattlesnake oil." Occasionally an observer of saddles in the cow country will see the cantle of one covered with a rattlesnake skin. Sometimes the skin will be for ornament; sometimes to ward off rheumatism.

James Bell, who went with a herd of cattle from San Antonio to California in 1854 and kept a diary, has this entry: "June 6 — Found an hombre skinning three rattlesnakes. When I inquired the use he would put their skins to, he told me that by stretching the skin on the cantle of the saddle no harm would come to my posteriors, i.e., no galls or sores; also that by fastening a piece of the skin between my hat and the lining I never would have the headache. The hombre took the fat out of the snakes and divided it with those who had faith in its virtues. It is good for wounds of various kinds. The Mexican gave me a very large snakeskin. . . . I stretched it tightly on the cantle, covering it entirely, and used the end for covering the horn."

The dust from rattlesnake rattles was supposed to make one go blind if it got into one's eyes, though the rattles carried in a hatband would prevent headache. I have heard that rattlesnake rattles are also excellent for babies to cut their teeth on, though six-shooter cartridges are said to be just as good. In the cedar brakes that look down upon the dome of the Texas capitol, some of the woodchoppers sew the skeleton of a rattlesnake up in an old sock and wear it around the neck; in addition to warding off rheumatism this talisman will bring as much good luck as a rabbit's foot.

Many a fiddler has kept rattles in his fiddle in order to prevent the strings from getting damp. This practice is probably based on the belief that a rattlesnake never allows his own "musical box" to get wet. Perhaps the belief has foundation, as evidenced by the two big rattlesnakes I once saw disporting themselves in a pool of water, and all the while keeping their rattles turned up high and dry.

Cowboys' Respect for Rattlesnakes

The old saying that familiarity breeds contempt does not apply to rattlesnakes. I have known many men who virtually gave up hunting on account of a growing fear of rattlesnakes. I have seen it stated in print that cowboys make a practice of seizing rattlesnakes by the tail and popping their heads off. I myself have never witnessed such a stunt, though I have seen a coachwhip's head popped off. Nevertheless, I know from reliable witnesses that a few old-time cowboys were foolhardy enough to pop the head off rattlesnakes. The stunt was rare, however, and I am sure it was not attempted on the giant rattlers of southern Texas, which sometimes weigh as much as twenty-five pounds.

I know one thing. Let a crowd of cowhands be bedding down for the night around the chuck wagon amid some scraggly bushes and then let the rattling of a snake be heard somewhere in the vicinity. You will witness a stampede that no herd of Longhorns ever surpassed for instantaneous celerity, some of the men dragging their beds with them but none of them stopping until well out of hearing distance. And the next morning it will be daylight before the cook gets close enough to his box to boil coffee.

The fact that men of the range usually kill rattlesnakes with either a quirt or a rope, which is doubled or knotted, does not mean that they are contemptuous of them; it means that they have the striking power of rattlesnakes nicely gauged. And it is an unwritten law that whoever sees a rattler will kill it.

Accounts of rattlesnakes crawling under the blankets of campers are not infrequent. "One of the most painful occurrences of this kind that I heard of," relates an Englishman who ranched in the West some years, "happened to two brothers, cowboys. They were sleeping under the same blankets, and as the night air was sharp, they had drawn the covering up over their heads. They slept so soundly that they did not notice when a rattlesnake crawled to the top of their upper blanket and settled himself to sleep in the hollow between their bodies. Towards morning, thinking it was time to get up, the elder brother put his head out from below the bedding. The first thing he saw was their dangerous bedfellow, swollen out with anger, coiling himself up and preparing to strike. Instantly he withdrew his head under the protection of the blankets, at the same time shouting to his brother, 'Look out!' His poor brother, taking the words literally, did look out, and was immediately bitten by the snake, both in the face and once in the neck. He quickly died from the effects."

I can believe the story, though if the morning were very cool, a rattlesnake would be torpid. Evidence that rattlesnakes sometimes crawl into the bed of a sleeper-out is unimpeachable; however, they are likely to crawl under some loose portion of the pallet rather than into the bed itself.

The Rattlesnake and His Enemies

The rattlesnake has many enemies besides man. The one about which the most stories have been told is the paisano, known also as the chaparral cock, roadrunner, and bird of paradise. "Bird of paradise, you say," replied the stranger who got that name in answer to a query. "Well, he is a hell of a long ways from home." Nobody else has told the paisano-rattlesnake yarn so well as Alfred Henry Lewis, in *Wolfville*, a collection of narratives supposed to be laid around old Tombstone, Arizona.

While running across the desert one day, two roadrunners, denominated for convenience Bill and Jim, discovered a rattlesnake asleep under a soapweed bush.

"Tharupon," relates the Old Cattleman of Wolfville, "these yere roadrunners turns in mighty diligent; an' not makin' no more noise than shadows, they go pokin' out on the plains ontil they finds a flat cactus which is dead, so they can tear off the leaves with their bills. . . . One after the other, Jim an' Bill teeters up, all silent, with a flat cactus leaf in their beaks, an' starts to fence in the rattlesnake. They builds a corral of cactus all about him, which the same is mebby six foot across. Them engineering feats takes Jim an' Bill twenty minutes. But they completes 'em; an' thar's the rattlesnake, plumb surrounded. . . .

"Jim an' Bill knows the rattlesnake can't cross this thorny corral. He don't look it none, but from the way he plays his hand, I takes it a rattlesnake is sensitive an' easy hurt onder the chin.

"No sooner is the corral made, than Jim an' Bill, without a word of warnin', opens up a war jig 'round the outside, flappin' their pinions and screechin' like squaws. Nacherally the rattlesnake wakes up. The sight of them two roadrunners cussin' an' swearin' at him, an' carryin' on that away scares him. . . .

"He buzzes an' quils up, an' onsheaths his fangs, an' makes bluffs to strike Bill an' Jim, but they only hops an' dances about, thinkin' up more ornery things to say. Every time the rattlesnake goes to crawl away — which he does frequent — he strikes the cactus thorns an' pulls back. By an' by he sees he's elected, an' he gets that enraged he swells up till he's big as two snakes. At last comes the finish, an' matters gets dealt down to the turn. The rattlesnake suddenly crooks his neck, he's so plumb locoed with rage an' fear, an' socks his fangs into himse'f. That's the fact; bites himse'f, an' never lets up till he's dead."

Another "authority" says that after the paisano corrals

his victim with thorns he drops some particularly sharp ones amidst the coils of the rattler, which in its writhing squeezes them into its flesh and soon becomes so agonized that it bites itself and dies.

In *The Cowboy*, a scientific treatise of merit, Philip Ashton Rollins gives yet another twist to the paisano's war tactics. "The chaparral cock might stop his hunt for bugs, seize in its bill a group of cactus thorns, spread its wings wide and low, and, running more speedily than any race-horse, dodging as elusively as does the heat lightning, drive those thorns squarely into the snake's open mouth, peck out both the beady eyes, and then resume the hunt for bugs."

As a matter of fact, the paisano is so fond of the flesh of lizards and snakes that if he captures one he can be counted upon to devour it. Beyond all doubt, the paisano kills rattlesnakes, but how big a one he will attack is problematical. Nor do I know how far to credit the belief that rattlesnakes fear thorns. In the brush country the mockingbird often builds its nest so that the outside bristles with an armor of thorns; this, according to popular belief, is a defense against snakes. Although rattlesnakes take refuge amid thickly growing prickly pear and often go into thorn-studded rat dens, those I have observed avoid contact with thorns.

I have one bit of evidence to offer bearing on the belief that the paisano finds the rattlesnake asleep and fences him in with thorns. Captain Bill Sterling, one time adjutant-general of the state of Texas, was reared in the brush. One day, so he related to me, a Mexican came to him and took him to see a queer thing. It was the skeleton of a rattlesnake almost totally surrounded by a small, irregular corral of thorns, most of them of prickly pear. The thorns, like the snake, had been there a long time; the "fence" was probably an inch and a half or two inches high. For my part, I know that herpetologists have not yet been cut enough in the thorns with paisanos and rattlesnakes to settle this so-called "folk belief."

An observer not prone to embroider facts describes a contest between a paisano and a "good-sized" rattler thus. The paisano dashed at the snake and whirled just at the instant the less agile snake struck; then, before the snake could recoil for another strike, the bird on the run pecked him back of the head. These maneuvers were repeated until the paisano killed the reptile.

While the belief that hogs are immune to snake poison is pure superstition, hogs — and javelinas (peccaries) likewise — kill rattlesnakes for food. Percy G. Ebbutt, a squatter of the last century who wrote a very sober and generally dull book entitled *Emigrant Life in Kansas*, tells of a relationship between rattlesnakes and hogs that is quite novel.

"On one occasion," he says, "Humphrey went out to feed the hogs, and upon looking into the sty occupied by the old sow and her family of ten, he found a rattlesnake lying with the busy little ones taking some refreshment.

They all seemed very happy together, with the exception of one poor little fellow, who was of course crowded out.

"Humphrey called us to see this curious sight, and then the snake was dragged out and killed with a pitchfork. Some people may doubt the accuracy of this statement, and I almost think that I should, had I not seen it myself. I had heard before of cows being milked by snakes, but not pigs, as the two are mortal enemies; but in this case the old sow was asleep, or she would not have allowed it."

Later (page 190) there is a story about a wild turkey fighting a rattlesnake. I believe, too, this statement, made by August Santleben in *A Texas Pioneer:*

"Traveling the road near Uvalde," he says, "I saw a large flock of wild turkeys in an open glade near the highway. I stopped when I saw the gobblers congregated in a circle where they seemed to be fighting, but I soon perceived that they were killing a large rattlesnake. One after the other would spring into the air in rapid succession and come down on the reptile, which they struck a hard blow with one wing that might have been heard quite a distance. Apparently all the gobblers took part in the fracas, and they appeared to be greatly excited, but the hens fed quietly in the vicinity and seemed to be indifferent to what was going on.

"I watched them about ten minutes before they observed my presence and became alarmed. After they disappeared in the brush I approached the glade and found the snake coiled up and almost dead. Evidently the gobblers had been engaged in killing him for some time before I appeared on the scene, and if they had not been disturbed, the victim would have provided a feast for the whole flock, because it was their custom to eat the snakes killed in that way."

The late J. F. Barnes told me that rattlesnakes on his ranch in San Saba County were greatly diminished by hundreds of domestic turkeys that he allowed a man to range on his land.

I cannot leave the topic of rattlesnake enemies without quoting one of the many marvels recorded by old John Brickell in his rare book entitled *The Natural History of North Carolina*, first printed in 1737.

Tortoises, says Brickell, "are mortal Enemys to the Rattlesnakes, killing them wherever they meet, which they do by catching the Snake a little below the Neck, and so draw his Head into their Shell, which makes the Snake beat his Tail, and twist about with all the strength and violence imaginable to get away, but the Terebin soon dispatches him, by pressing him to Death between his Shells, and there leaves him."

Snake Fights

"Well," said the old rancher, "I saw something once concerning rattlesnakes that I never expect to see again. It was out in the Davis Mountains country and I was just a kid. One day I rode up on two rattlesnakes swallowing each other. Each was about three feet long and they had each other by the tail. They had swallowed so far that each snake was actually beginning to swallow itself. I sat there on my horse watching them maybe fifteen minutes, and all the time the hoop they made was getting smaller and smaller. After a while I got down and killed them. I have always regretted that I did not let them finish swallowing and then bring them in to preserve in alcohol. They would be quite a curiosity."

Personally I have no doubt that they would have gone on swallowing until nothing but the heads were left and the circle had been reduced to a dot. Any of the higher mathematicians that figure on infinity can understand the proposition. Why, it is Einsteinism applied to rattlesnakes. I told the old rancher that his observation reminded me of the two wildcats fighting. Every time one of them jumped on the other, the one under jumped out and mounted the one that had been on top. Exchanging positions that way, they kept getting higher and higher until the man watching lost sight of them and would have doubted that they were still progressively fighting if he had not noticed an occasional bit of fur falling at his feet.

There are many accounts of combats between rattlesnakes, and, as these creatures are no better tempered than men or other animals, it can hardly be doubted that they do fight. But whether such a combat, as it is claimed, inevitably brings death to victor and vanquished alike, I do not know. It is agreed that the rattlers attempt to bite each other and generally succeed, but there has been much controversy as to whether rattlesnake poison is deadly to a rattlesnake itself.

If the poison is poisonous to the poisoner, then it might seem that any prey bitten by it would convey the poison and thus death to its devourer. The fact is that in order to be effective the poison must enter the blood. A man may without injury to himself, provided his internal organs are healthy, swallow a large amount of rattlesnake venom. Presumably a rattlesnake can do the same thing. Again, the rattler does not always inject poison into its victims; sometimes, like other snakes, it constricts its prey. Then, there are accounts not yet disproved of creatures so charmed that they submitted to being swallowed without being either bitten or constricted. Finally there is the story of the mole.

"Some flat-boatmen on one occasion captured a large blacksnake in the Tallahatchie River, and put it in a cage. . . . Accidentally finding a mole, about the size of a mouse, they put 'the groundling' into the snake's cage. The reptile at once gulped it down, but the mole, making no difference between the sides of its prison-house and the solid earth, much to the astonishment of the flat-boatmen, ate its way out of the snake's side: whereupon it was swallowed again, and again gnawed its way into daylight." The process was repeated three times before the snake, utterly exhausted, gave up mole-swallowing as an unprofitable business.

The king snake, the blacksnake, and the coachwhip are

all credited with being enemies of rattlesnakes, and the credence seems to be fully substantiated. Because a black-snake and a rattlesnake put in a cage together do not fight is no proof that they never fight. Each can go for months without eating. A bird has been put in a cage with a rattle-snake and left there for months without being molested; yet it is well known that rattlesnakes eat birds.

Obstinate Questionings

John Burroughs was, I suppose, the last naturalist to hope that he might some day witness a brood of little snakes scurrying into the protective "innards" of their dam. Nevertheless, many men yet alive *know* that they have seen this very thing — see the chapter beginning on page 152. Such accounts might be multiplied indefinitely. The myth has been treated of extensively by scholars.

While country people keep alive the belief that snakes swallow their young, it was not they who started the fallacy that rattlesnakes, "dogtown owls," and prairie dogs all live together happily in holes. If he gets a chance, a rattlesnake will certainly swallow a young owl or prairie dog, but any dog hole he lives in is abandoned, the dogs and owls going either out of it or into the snake. Just here I draw from the observant Oscar Rush.

"A rattlesnake is very much afraid of a herd of cattle when they pass over him. He has inherited the knowledge that should one of those sharp hoofs be planted upon him he is cut in two. He does not coil up in position to strike, warning by rattling, as if to say, 'Do not tread on me.' He simply runs like a scared wolf, and goes into the first hole he sees, no matter to whom it belongs. If he goes into a live prairie-dog hole, he comes out as soon as the danger is past. If he does not do so, the dog and all his neighbors will gather at the mouth of his hole and cork it up, by filling earth in with their paws and tamping it with their noses so hard that the snake cannot get out, and he will starve. Should you ever see a dog hole so sealed, you may know that it is the grave of Mr. Rattler."

Nor does the rattlesnake, as is commonly believed, always rattle before he strikes. The ground camouflages the rattlesnake so perfectly, however, that it is exceedingly fortunate he does generally give to any passerby a warning of his presence. Asa Jones, a ranchman, about whom I have written in *Cow People*, told me of a curious coincidence illustrative of a rattlesnake's failure to rattle. He and another man were riding a piece of fence together. Jones was on a bronc from which he could not conveniently dismount. When they came to a broken wire, the other man, who had a gentle horse, dismounted to repair it. While the other man was down on his knee splicing the wire, Jones saw an extra-large rattler striking at him. The snake had not rattled once, but began rattling while in the act of striking. His open mouth was stopped by the strand of wire, the lower jaw passing under it and the upper jaw over it.

Indian Ways with Rattlesnakes

Reports that rattlesnakes make good eating are not base-less. Many white men have eaten rattlesnake flesh fried, and the Indians of various tribes often used it to compound the famously delectable boudin blanc. A man who as a boy was captive among the Comanches and Apaches describes their use of rattlesnake meat.

"The soup we had may not strike the fancy of civilized people, but I learned to like it and considered it a rare treat when the squaws prepared it for us. They would take the paunch of a buffalo and wash it out, and if they could find a big rattlesnake they would kill him before he was disturbed so as to prevent him from biting himself. Then they would cut off his head about twelve inches back and cut off the tail, taking the middle part and boiling it until the flesh dropped off the bones. The meat, which is almost snow white, tastes very much like fish. They would put this snake meat inside the buffalo paunch, together with some choice buffalo meat, wild onions, wild potatoes, and other wild vegetables, the names of which I have forgotten, to which had been added about two gallons of water. . . . Then, after tying up both ends of the paunch, they would put it in a big kettle and boil it. When done it would be as large as a bucket, and it would keep for a long time. Sometimes we would lay that paunch on the fire and it would swell and grow until it seemed ready to burst; then we would take it off and open it and have hot soup ready to serve. It was good. When the contents were all eaten, we would often gamble to see who would get the paunch, which itself was delicious."

Finally it is interesting to remember that the rattlesnake is the cynosure of the snake dance made world-famous by the Hopi Indians of Arizona — "the most astounding barbaric ceremonial civilized eyes have ever looked upon." Much has been written on the ceremonial by both scientists and popular journalists. Yet the power of the dancers over the giant rattlers that they carry in their mouths and hands and the methods by which they make themselves apparently immune to snakebite are still unknown.

C. B. Ruggles, who was for fifteen years intimate with the Hopis and several times witnessed their rites, saw and heard some things that seem worth putting down. According to the story certain Hopis told Ruggles, the rites began a long, long time ago following twelve successive years of drouth. During these awful years the Hopis now and then got a little cornmeal by trading with distant tribes; what they got was very dear and very sacred. The prophet of the Hopis told them the drouth came from the fact that they had been abusing the snakes. They must go north towards the blue light, west towards the yellow light, south towards the white light, and east towards the red light and bring in snakes, wash them, put sacred meal on them, and pray for rain.

Since that first ceremony so long ago the villages of the Hopis have every other year danced the dance of the deadly snakes, though nonpoisonous snakes as well as poisonous ones are used. To determine the date on which it is to be danced the chiefs of a typical village stand on a certain peak that looks west through a narrow "saddle" between two mesas and watch for the night when the moon sets exactly in the center of that saddle. This is in late August or early September. Exactly sixteen days later, near sunset, the weird ceremonial is accomplished. During that period the dancers of the Snake Fraternity have fasted and purified themselves, and the sacred snakes have been gathered together.

On the final day the snakes are sprinkled with meal and washed with water from the little spring that nearly went dry during the great drouth. Then there is a brief action in the ceremony that Ruggles was not permitted to see. After the ceremony, during which he saw more than one man bitten in the face, Ruggles caught a large rattler that had been released away from the village — for the snakes are taken north, west, south, and east and turned loose. He examined it closely and upon "milking" its fangs was able to extract only a drop or two. He thinks that during the interval he was not permitted to see the Snake Men, they extracted the venom, though not the fangs, from the snakes. However, it must be remembered that these performers before they subject themselves to the fangs have undergone a rigorous fast and that immediately thereafter they take an emetic. Various desert herbs have been pointed out as providing antivenin used by the Hopis, but laboratory analyses have failed to discover any properties in them that would antidote rattlesnake poison. Why the Hopis are not injured by rattlesnake bites is still a moot question.

An enormous tome might be compiled of the tales hereditary among the American Indians in which the rattlesnake plays a part. One from the Cherokees, preserved by a missionary who lived among them for twenty years, will illustrate the point of view of the aborigine, who invariably identified himself with nature — a "brother" not only to the ox but to the rattlesnake. The missionary's story follows:

On one occasion while riding with my interpreter, I overtook Blanket on foot. I walked my horse by his side for the purpose of conversation. While thus engaged we discovered a venomous serpent coiled by the side of the narrow path. I observed Blanket turn aside to avoid the serpent, and I requested the interpreter to get down and kill it. He did so, and I then inquired of Blanket why he did not kill the serpent. He answered, "I never kill snakes, and so the snakes never kill me; I will tell you all about it when you next come to see me."

Soon after, I visited the old man and he redeemed his promise with the following story:

"When I was a young man," said he, "one of my young companions killed a rattlesnake. The next day I went out to hunt, and my way led through a part of the forest very much infested with venomous serpents; in one place to avoid stepping upon a snake, I walked upon a fallen pine. As I approached the end of the log, I discovered a snake coiled on it and reared to strike. As I drew near, he bowed and accosted me in friendly and very respectful terms, and told me he was sent to invite me to the residence of his tribe. I followed, but at a safe distance. After going a few yards, he came to a perpendicular rock fifteen feet high and extending many rods in length. At the point where he approached the rock there was a seam. He turned the tip of his tail to this seam, and the rock began to open till the aperture was as wide as the door of a human dwelling. He invited me very politely to enter, which I did with much trepidation. The aperture closed after me, and egress was now impossible, unless my singular conductor would please open the way for me.

"I was much alarmed, but my guide, with accents of kindness and respect, told me to dismiss all fear, for I was in no danger. Thus assured, I began to explore this subterranean abode of the serpent race. I found myself in a vast hall some ten yards wide and hundreds of yards long. It was illuminated by a large council fire around which the whole tribe of snakes was assembled. Near the fire was stretched a dead rattlesnake. The chief of the tribe, a rattlesnake larger around than my body, and at least thirty feet long, told me to look upon the dead snake, and say whether or not I knew it. I did so, and recognized the rattlesnake killed by my companion the day before. The father and mother and all the near kindred of the dead

[48]

snake were making great lamentation over it. After all had taken a last look at their murdered companion, his lifeless body was borne away.

"A solemn council was then holden to decide how his death should be avenged. Several eloquent speeches were made, in which the virtues of their murdered companion were set forth for the imitation of his survivors, and the loss sustained by the community was deeply deplored. The question was then put by the patriarch of the race: What punishment shall be inflicted upon the murderer? Let him be put to death, was the unanimous response of the whole council. In what manner shall he be put to death? Let him be bitten in the heel by one of our number. Who will carry this righteous sentence into execution? . . . Every eye was directed to an individual who had shown himself especially affected by the death of his murdered comrade. The individual thus tacitly appealed to presented himself before the patriarch and said: 'I am the eldest brother of the dead. Within seven days I will infuse the deadly venom, with which the Creator has armed us, into the heel of the murderer.'

"A hiss of approbation, accompanied by a concert of all the rattles of the assembled multitude, indicated the favorable reception of his speech; and forthwith the council broke up. My conductor now beckoned me to follow him, and I gladly complied. On our way out he inquired what I thought of the decision of the council. I could but acknowledge that it was evenhanded justice, and in accordance with our customs in similar circumstances. Arrived at the place of egress, my guide applied his tail, as before, to the seam in the rock, and soon an opening was made, and he very politely bade me farewell and bowed me out. I rejoiced once more to behold the light of day, to see the sunny hills, and to breathe the balmy air; but my spirits were too deeply depressed to pursue the chase. I returned to my cabin.

"Soon I sought the habitation of my friend, and related to him all I had witnessed in the cavern of snakes, and besought him to keep in his cabin and not expose himself to the fatal decree which had been passed against his life. He laughed and said he was not a child to be frightened by the tales of a pretended prophet. A few days later he was playing ball with the young men of his village. His opponent sent the ball beyond the open acre prepared for the game into a thicket of low bushes. He ran to get the ball; and just as he stooped to pick it up, a large rattlesnake struck its fangs into his heel. He called to us that he was bitten by a rattlesnake. We hastened to his assistance and brought him into the open playground. He was fearfully swollen and in the most excruciating pain; before we could procure any antidote, he was dead. Thus was the decree of the snake council executed, and the murder of a rattlesnake avenged.

"And now," concluded Blanket, "you know why I never kill snakes, and why snakes never kill me."

Some Rattlesnakes I've Associated With

DESPITE ALL THE FEARS of summer vacationists, I'm glad that rattlesnakes exist. I was born among them, grew up among them, and have, over the years, encountered them in many places. In a piece entitled "Peaceful Coexistence with Rattlesnakes" in *Harper's* magazine, the writer, who owns a summer place in the Catskills, seems indignant that neither the federal government nor the state operates a bureau to exterminate rattlesnakes. He simply can't resort to the Catskills without "steering clear of unexplored woods, rocky ledges and ravines." In other words, he feels more in place on pavement than on the good earth.

Country people, in Texas at least, and many townspeople used to keep their yards absolutely bare of grass. Comparatively few cultivated flowers relieved the bareness. The explanation, I suppose, is that grass might harbor snakes. We boys used to keep our yard on a ranch in Live Oak County clear of all weeds, stray grasses and leaves; the violets, roses, chrysanthemums, cape jessamine, honeysuckle, trumpet vine and other flowers being, as

Byron said of man's love, "a thing apart." I have a basket woven by an Opata Indian woman in Sonora called, on account of its design, "Snake-in-the-Grass." Looked at in one way, a diamondback rattlesnake zigzags plainly amid geometric lines; then it disappears and all is geometric design. One of the proverbial epithets for a deceitful person is "snake-in-the-grass."

As a matter of fact, rattlesnakes are far more often found on bare ground than in grass. One may be in scraggly grass along a trail traveled by rodents, but I never expect to find one out on green grass. A rattlesnake would be more conspicuous on a clipped green sward than on sand, rocks, or brown earth, where its camouflage is perfect. The "grass snake" has lines that blend with green grass, over which it lightly glides. Most of the rattlers are earthen-hued. Water moccasins and other snakes that lurk along water go into green grass, sedges and weeds to waylay frogs. The typical rattler is as dryland as the "dryland terrapin." He swims on occasion, keeping his rattles dry. A Mexican name for him is cola seca (dry tail).

One day I picked up a Mexican in Austin, Texas, to do a day's work on my Paisano place in the hills. Another laborer got him for me. I didn't like his looks when I saw him. I soon found out that he was worthless. I put him to pulling up cockleburs in a creek valley. He was afraid to move out of a trail. In the afternoon I saw him thrashing tall green grass; he explained that he was trying to run the snakes out of it before he'd go into it and pull out a few cockleburs. I've been sorry ever since that I paid him anything for his time; I can't say for his work, for he didn't do any. His fear of rattlesnakes was as unrealistic as the government's policy of putting his kind on "unemployed" relief.

On the ranch of my boyhood we frequently killed rattlesnakes in the yard or under the house and out in the pasture, but the first particular rattlesnake I have a recollection of is one I found as a barefooted boy up Long Hollow, where my father and another man were repairing a windmill. Actually they pulled the pipe out of the well to repack the pump. Playing around, I saw a rattlesnake coiled on dark ground maybe twenty-five steps away from the windmill. I called to Papa, going towards him. He came and said, "Where is the snake?" I couldn't see it and was walking around looking for it when he said, "Jump this way!" The coiled snake was within two or three feet of where I was standing. It was not rattling or striking, but of course it was killed.

Another particular snake, which appeared several years later, gave me a more distinct feeling, I won't say of fear, but of strong belligerence and antipathy. I had ridden down to the Ramirez waterhole in Ramirenia Creek after dark. My horse was drinking and I was about to get down to drink also when a rattlesnake set up a furious rattling. My horse lunged back. I didn't know where the snake was

[53]

and had no impulse to get down and try to find him. After that I often had that feeling of antagonism, my hackles rising at hearing a rattlesnake rattle.

One time we drove a small herd of steers to Mathis to ship in railroad cars. We made camp close to the shipping pens, having arrived late, so as to be on hand for an early train. When the men saddled up about daylight, after breakfast, one found a small rattler under his saddle, which had been thrown on the ground. That snake didn't create nearly as much ruckus as one did in camp over on the Aransas Creek one night. We had been branding yearlings all day and came to the wagon about dark. After we had eaten supper and were about to spread our pallets, a rattlesnake set up a buzzing in the midst of us. Flashlights were then unknown. Nobody knew where the snake was. The hands scattered like a covey of quail, each with his bedding, and no sleep was lost.

I have never camped with anybody who took the trouble to coil a hair rope, a cabestro, around his pallet to ward off snakes. Some people in some parts of the country believed to an extent in its efficacy, the theory being that a rattlesnake does not like to have his belly tickled by horsehairs and so won't crawl over a hair rope, one of horse tail being more prickly than one of horse mane. The theory was long ago proven invalid. One summer on a story-hunting excursion into New Mexico, I stopped at Vernon to visit Bob More, ornithologist and manager of the widespread Waggoner ranches. He insisted on my taking a hair rope hanging in his office. I delighted in the gift but never used it as a defense against night-crawling rattlesnakes. People who live with rattlesnakes take them for granted, though they watch out for them.

One time on a warm winter day I was riding in the sacahuiste — tall salt grass growing in clumps — in the Nueces River Valley on my uncle Jim Dobie's Olmos ranch in La Salle County. The sun was low. I was riding almost due east when I heard off to the northeast the loudest rattlesnake rattling I recollect having heard. My horse shied, and looking to where the sound was coming from, I saw an enormous rattlesnake reared up fully two feet high between clumps of grass. I guess he was on the prod and wanted to tell any passerby not to come his way. I really wasn't going his way at all when he rattled. Rattlesnakes are said to have almost no hearing but to be acutely sensitive to motion on the ground. I rode up fairly close to him and pulled a thirty-thirty out of the scabbard and killed him. At times I have regretted killing that particular rattlesnake, for rattlesnakes add to the interest of the brush country as almost no other animal. I gave this one a poor reward for the vivid memory he gave me.

Maybe the nearest I ever came to being bitten was on LaMota ranch, which joined the Olmos. My wife Bertha was with me, and we rode in a car to an earthen tank, where I got out just to look around. I was on top of a wide dam not too far away from the car when I heard a scream. I moved in a hurry. Bertha told me that she'd seen a rattlesnake strike at me and miss, the strike being the fastest action in the animal world she'd ever seen. I'm positive this rattlesnake did not rattle before it struck, or I should have heard it. It struck while or after I was passing it — and was manifestly a poor judge of distance.

Another time I was with my wife on a dude ranch in Medina County. We had ridden out horseback and dismounted to look around. She was walking toward a bird, and just as she got between two oak trees and looked down became aware of a rattlesnake coiled almost at her feet. It didn't rattle and it didn't strike. Naturally she got away from it.

While a flour peddler was governor of Texas — backed by certain rich oil men to cut the throat of the New Deal and voted for by tens of thousands of people because they considered him such a "good man" (he habitually advertised over the radio every Sunday morning where he was going to "worship") — I was driving along a rough pasture road in the hills west of Austin. Across a shackly fence that I could have very easily crawled through, I saw a big rattlesnake moving leisurely off. My hackles did not rise as they have risen on many occasions at sight of a rattlesnake. I stopped the car, got out and looked at this specimen. I realized that I had much rather be in his presence than that of a hypocritical, ignorant pretender to piety and statesmanship. I addressed him thus: "Fellow citizen, you belong to the ground; you have never pretended to belong anywhere else. You can be trusted to fang your prey and kill it with poison. You can also be trusted not to lie. I prefer being in your company to being in that of the governor of the state of Texas. Go on about your business, and I'll go on about mine. Adiós."

I recollect one particular snake on account of the strong odor it gave off. Along in 1921 while I was managing the Olmos ranch in La Salle County, I went to the Piedra tank to meet a string of steers that the cow outfit was bringing from another pasture. Up on a rise of ground maybe two hundred yards from the tank a goatherder had his camp and brush pens in which the goats were enclosed at night to protect them from coyotes. The camp ground was distinctly smelly, but the smells were not quite so strong down by the tank. I arrived an hour or so before the steers got there and part of the time sat on the ground near the trunk of a long-fallen mesquite tree. While I was sitting there, idle-minded, I was aroused by a strong smell — distinctly different from that made by billygoats. I can't say what it was like. It alerted me, and looking about in search of its origin, I saw a big rattlesnake, fully five feet long, not more than four steps away, approaching the other end of the log. He was in slow motion and apparently not alarmed. The odor I detected was coming from him. I got the rope off my saddle, doubled it and killed him. I had rather kill a rattlesnake with a doubled rope, particularly with a knot tied in it, than with a chunk of wood or a rock. It's more easily wielded. After I struck the snake the odor became heavier — more intense.

In his book *The Sense of Smell*, Roy Bedichek devotes a chapter to the odors that rattlesnakes do, or do not, give off. One rattlesnake hunter describes the smell of a quiet rattlesnake as that of a green watermelon just cut open, but of an angry or aroused rattlesnake as similar to that of a wet dog. Another witness identifies the smell as resembling that of a split cucumber; another as suggesting the smell of a billygoat. Another one asserts that he never smelled a rattlesnake before he found it and does not believe anybody else could smell a snake before finding it. The most ignorant are always the most positive. If a dog can find a rattlesnake by smelling it out, and some dogs can, I don't see why a keen-nosed human being might not find one through the sense of smell. I am not keen-nosed; I have smoked too many pounds of pipe tobacco. No smoker can be keen-nosed. One time down in the mountains of western Sonora I hunted javelinas with a native hombre del campo. He had a couple of worthless dogs and smelled a bunch of five javelinas before the dogs did. He told me later that he had located rattlesnakes by smell. I've smelled several other rattlesnakes, but the one at the Piedra tank was the only one I ever smelled before I saw or heard it.

Not in belief, but merely following folk superstition, as a boy I hung various dead rattlesnakes up on fences or bushes or left them turned on their backs "to make it rain." We always needed rain. It used to be thought, perhaps still is, that if a dead rattlesnake is left where it was killed, its mate would come to it. I've kept an eye on quite a few dead rattlesnakes to see if the mate appeared, but never saw one appear.

One dead rattlesnake in my experience stands out. As a boy I was riding horseback alone out in what we called the Big Pasture of our ranch in Live Oak County. Approaching a fringe of brush, I saw three deer under a clump of live oak trees up an open hill. A doe was jumping up and down, coming down stiff-legged as if hoofing something. I stopped and watched the performance for a minute or more before the deer scented me and dashed away. Then I rode to where the doe had been jumping up and down stiff-legged and saw a rattlesnake, dead but still writhing, its hide lacerated in several places. I've always heard that deer sometimes kill rattlesnakes. I saw this. On the other hand, the most deer I've seen in the brush country of southwest Texas have been where rattlesnakes were also most abundant. I doubt if deer kill many rattlesnakes.

One time I saw twelve or fifteen wild turkey gobblers making a great to-do over something on the ground in brush. I thought it must be a rattlesnake they were after, but when I got there I couldn't find any rattlesnake — dead or alive.

I'm inclined not to believe many things heard and read about rattlesnakes. Years ago I ran a series of newspaper columns on the subject: "Do Rattlesnakes Swallow Their Young?" Scores of people wrote to inform me of seeing rattlesnakes and other species of snakes swallow little ones (see the chapter beginning on page 152 for some of the narratives). Many people see whatever they expect to see, believe what they want to believe. If they are brought up to look for ghosts, they'll see ghosts. If they expect to find a robber, a devil, or a communist hiding under a bed, they are sure to find him; at least, they will report the finding. In society and in many newspapers any kind of rumor about any kind of beast and often about innocent people is spread abroad. I'm no longer actively interested in superstitions and rumors about rattlesnakes. Yet any really good story about a rattlesnake is justified.

I pretend to no scientific knowledge concerning snakes; my outdoor experience with them, mostly in the brush country of southern Texas, has been only casual. I shall go on looking for something. I repeat that I affirm nothing, that I merely transmit. Some folklore has an interest in itself, whether it leads to any general truth or not. I make an end now by reprinting the introduction to a newspaper article I wrote immediately after the senatorial election, by the Democratic Party, in Texas in August, 1942.

I grew up understanding that a man even halfway decent would always shut any gate he had opened to go through and would always kill any rattlesnake he got a chance at. Well, just yesterday I went out into the hills and came face to face with a rattlesnake. I had shut all the gates before I met him, and I shut all the gates after I met him. He was a big one, and when he rattled and I got a whiff of his odor — apt to be strong in the dog days of August — the blood rushed up into the back of my head just as many a rattlesnake has sent it rushing.

But I didn't even try to find a stick to kill him. I stood still and watched him glide off into an old badger hole under some cedars. While the hair was getting stiff on the back of my head I had two thoughts that caused my inaction. In the first place, despite my instinctive revulsion, that rusty old rattler suddenly appeared to me as something natural, native, and honest belonging to the land that I belonged to — a fellow creature that, after all, I would not want to see exterminated.

In the second place, it came to me how honest he is with his poison, not even the gleam of a manufactured smile on his face. He never lies about that poison, pretending that he is holy. The bloodcurdling, sinister music that he makes is not to beguile people into taking it as a rosy promise. No, that music is not a lie to conceal personal motives. There is not a fraudulent note in it. Even a person who had never learned the alphabet could read its meaning. It advertises plainly the poison behind it. It warns every listener to beware of poison. It would be inhuman to admire poison, but right there I conceived a kind of respect for poison that is honest about itself.

I may revert to my raising and kill the next rattlesnake I meet, but I knew one mighty good man who would not kill a rattlesnake under any condition. That was the noted hunter Ben V. Lilly. One cold, damp night while he was out on the trail of a bear in the Louisiana bottoms, he took refuge in a hollow cypress log and slept snug. About daylight he crawled out and made a fire right at the hollow. He roasted an ear of dry corn, and while he was eating it an immense rattlesnake, thawed out by the fire, ponderously crawled from where Lilly had spent the night.

Ben Lilly looked at him and said: "Brother, you didn't bother me last night. I went into your house and you let me be. I won't bother you now, and I promise you I won't ever bother any of your folks."

Being Casual with Rattlesnakes

NOBODY BROUGHT UP with rattlesnakes looks for them to the exclusion of everything else. A good observer doesn't see just one thing that he might be looking for. He sees things he's not looking for. I've seen city people out in the country become so concerned over rattlesnakes that they couldn't see the North Star on account of looking for them. I saw an advertisement just the other day by some concern offering leggins made of metal to be worn as insurance against rattlesnake bites.

In *The Adventures of Bigfoot Wallace*, by John C. Duval, the Little Author, who was riding along with Bigfoot, one day saw a rattlesnake. Bigfoot got down and killed it. "Captain," the Little Author asked, "how in the world have you managed to live so long and camp out so much at night in this wilderness without ever having been bitten by a rattlesnake?"

"Why, you see," Bigfoot answered, "if you don't lose your presence of mind, there's very little danger of a rattlesnake's biting you, even when he crawls to bed with you at night. When you discover one crawling under your blankets, all you've got to do is to lie still and let him fix himself to his notion (and they always pick out the warmest places), and as soon as he is fast asleep, you can jump up without the least danger of being bitten; but if you should move a peg before he has settled himself, he'll 'nip you' to a certainty."

This casual way of regarding rattlesnakes is very refreshing in contrast to the journalese screams that go up in attempts to bring the blood of readers to the boiling point. I have a letter from my friend Arthur Woodward that illustrates this casualness. In the fall of 1946 he went to the old A. B. Fall ranch near Three Rivers, south and east of Albuquerque, New Mexico, to examine certain petroglyphs chiseled in boulders.

Now I quote his words:

It was late afternoon when I reached the spot. As it began to grow dark I fumbled my way down the hill to the dirt road where I had left my car. Just before reaching it I heard a shot. As I was in a strange country, I moved onward with more caution. When the car came in sight I saw a man with a rifle standing beside it. He was a short, slender New Mexican.

He gave me "Buenas tardes" and introduced himself as Tomás Salazar, "a sus ordenes" [at your service]. Then in English he said, "I was hunting and saw your car standing here. When I got near I saw a snake coiled up right in front of it and I just killed it. You might have not seen it in the dark."

I thanked him and then asked him how far to the next town. I had my sleeping bag but was low on food. He said it was too far for me to go. Why not spend the night in his house? That sounded good; so we drove down to his wooden shack — a kitchen and one bedroom. He was a bachelor. When I got out he said: "Entrase mi casa con toda confianza." [Enter my house with entire confidence.]

Again I said "Muchas gracias" and went in. He offered me the bed, but I told him my sleeping bag was comfortable and with his permission I would bunk down on the kitchen floor. He demurred but finally said yes, although he assured me the bed was more comfortable. He also said it might be just as well to sleep inside the house because now and then big víboras de cascabeles crawled up on the porch during the night. I asked him if he had many snakes on his ranchito. "Sí, señor! Hay muchas."

Then he told me of his attempts at raising "cheekens" but the snakes caught and ate the little ones.

"Wan day," he related, "I went out to see if some of my leetle cheekens were still alive. Thees old gallina [hen] she had five or six pollitos which the hawks and the snakes had not caught. I hoped maybee I could keep them alive.

"There was one leetle cheeken what had no feathers. He was my leetle pela'o [pelado: hairless, featherless]. I tame heem and he follow me every place. Then wan by wan all

[65]

the leetle cheekens they disappear. I thought maybee a gavilán [hawk] which light sometimes on that beeg cottonwood had been catching the pollitos. So when all but my leetle pela'o had gone, he was lonesome and he follow right at my heels all the time. Sí, señor, just like a leetle puppy.

"I like my leetle pela'o and I say no gavilán gonna get you, mi pela'o. I carry my shotgun with me all the time. But never did I see that gavilán.

"Wan morning I went out to water mi caballo, and leetle pela'o was right at my heels. But when I got to the corral and looked around I didn't see mi pela'o. So I started back calling, 'Here, pela'o, here, pela'o,' but he didn't come. I look all around, but I didn't see any gavilán. Then I began poking under the bushes thinking maybee mi pela'o got scared and was hiding.

"Then, when I look under a big bush, there was wan damn beeg rattlesnake. I look closer and see a lump in his middle. So, I say, 'Eet was you, you beeg damn thief. You been catching my leetle cheekens, not that gavilán.' So, I blow hees head off and then I cut him open and there was my leetle pela'o.

"That is why, señor, I do not like these víboras de cascabeles. Mi pobrecito pela'o."

Snakes in the Corn Patch

"I HAVE KEPT QUIET all through your coyote yarns, panther yarns, javelina yarns, centipede yarns, and other yarns, but those snake stories out of Julius Caesar's time that you regaled us with on June 7 simply force me to relate some of my own snake stories — even if they are true." Thus begins a letter from John C. Myers of Eagle Pass, Texas. Everything from now on is in his words.

Thirty-eight years ago or so my people were farming in the western part of Wilson County. One year we had an especial amount of land planted in cotton, and it was up to my two brothers and me to keep it clean. Two neighbor boys were helping us chop a big block of cotton when Papa said that if we finished it by Saturday noon, he'd take us fishing down on the San Antonio River. All that Saturday morning we five boys flashed our long-handled hoes up and down the long cotton rows. It was a race to see who would reach the end of the last set of rows first and race on free.

I was out in front, leading the next boy by about thirty

[67]

feet, beating a perfect rhythm, eye on the row, and never watching where "me bare feet trod." Suddenly I stepped squarely on something squushy and yielding. My instant thought was a fresh cow chip. As I raised my hoe for another cut, the thought hit me, "There hasn't been a cow in this field since the last frost two months ago. It's a rattler." All this went through my head swifter than time can tell, while my foot was still set squarely over that old rattler. I let out a yell and left the ground with what my brothers still swear was a good ten-foot jump.

I never did see the snake, but I'd had an eyeful of snake during the long and terrible drouth just preceding the twenties. In that drouth some of the mesquites died and many wells went dry. Papa quit going to church because one Sunday the preacher in the course of a long prayer gave special thanks to the Supreme Being for sending us "that wonderful sunshine." Corn came up, got about three feet tall, tasseled out and died without forming an ear. Papa decided to cut runty corn for fodder. We boys would cut the cornstalks in the afternoons, using machetes, and pile the stalks in small bunches. Then, early in the mornings, while the night dampness was still on and before the dry fragile leaves shattered, we would gather the stalks into bundles and tie them securely with binder twine.

We knew that there were lots of rattlesnakes in the corn field, but armed as we were, we felt safe. In fact, we made quite a game of throwing machetes at rattlers and seeing who could cut the heads off closest to the neck.

One morning we were in the corn patch a little earlier than usual, before sunup, each with a bundle of twine cut into thirty-inch lengths, fastened to his belt so that a string at a time could easily be pulled out. Holding a piece of twine in the mouth like a calf-tying cowboy holding a pig-gin string, the boy gathered the cut cornstalks up until an armful was obtained; then, while compressing the bundle, he grabbed one end of the twine in one hand and, coming back around with the other end in the other hand, flung the bundle to the ground, where, with one knee on it, he tied it as tightly as possible so that it could stand when ended up in a shock with other bundles.

I had tied a few bundles loosely — still half asleep and half wet with the morning dew, when I saw the sun coming up square against me, between two rows of corn stubble. I gathered cornstalks slowly, looking at the newly risen sun, wondering how hot it would get by noon. I was lifting the bundle in my arms when the ugly flat head and about eleven inches of a big diamondback rattler poked up through the stalks and looked me squarely in the eye — his black forked tongue a-flickering my nose! Well . . . I scattered that bundle of fodder worse than a whirlwind scattering dry corn leaves as it meanders through a corn field. My excited yelping and swift exit from the patch caused my brothers to light out after me, but they never caught up until I was safe on the front gallery at home. After I had been sick, and had gotten my breath back, I got sick all over again, and it was some time before I got over the shakes. Our old mules had to get their sustenance from something else besides corn fodder that fall. We never tied another bundle of corn stalks that summer. Mama saw to that!

In any country abounding with poisonous snakes, there is always a certain amount of common knowledge about how to identify them. We learned early that poisonous snakes have flat heads and pits beneath their eyes.

One spring morning after a rain, when it was too wet for field work, Mama sent me to follow an old turkey hen that had hidden her nest down in the creek bottom. I was doing my best to stay unseen while keeping her in sight; she wouldn't go to her nest if aware that she was being followed. Sneaking through the brush and weeds, trying not to make any noise at all, imagining I was hot on the trail of a bunch of Mexican bandits, who were then making forays into Texas, I emerged from a thorny thicket into a natural clearing crossed by a cow trail. As I lay beside the trail picking out thorns and getting my breath back, I saw crawling across it a strange, beautiful, multicolored snake. It stopped about two feet from me, seemingly gentle. After making sure that its head was not flat, but round and pointed, I reached over and picked it up so as to study it better. It had to be a milk snake (commonly called garter snake, also king snake) since it had several colored bands.

While I was holding it in one hand and admiring it, it suddenly bent over and down and, on the back of my other hand, fanged two scratches about two inches in length, evenly spaced. They looked like scratches made from barbed wire. I flung that snake down quickly and stomped him, then licked the scratches. Considering the event ended, I began looking for our old turkey hen. Suddenly the poison hit me, and I found myself almost unable to breathe. In a few minutes I felt better, and then I lit out for home. In about five minutes I had another spell, only it was worse, and my heart almost quit. Mama treated my hand with home remedies while Papa cranked the old Ford up. Then we headed for town and the family doctor. On the two-hour trip I passed out several times. I had the utmost difficulty breathing, and could feel my heart almost come to a standstill; then the spasm would end, and I could breathe normally. I found out later that I had been bitten by a coral snake, the most deadly of our native poisonous snakes; I still have two latent scars that glow under a phosphorescent light.

After our kindhearted family doctor finished treating and dressing my hand, he said, "Son, why did you pick up that snake? Didn't you know that he might bite you?"

"Yes, sir," I replied, "but I didn't think he was poison. He did not have a flat head."

"Well," said Dr. Oxford, "I think you are the one that has the flat head."

[71]

The Rattlesnake Hunter

N ORMAN HESLEP of gas and oil fields in Texas and
Louisiana was tarrying in Houston, and hoping to
retire soon to an island in Caddo Lake, where he could
camp with birds, squirrels, possums and coons, when he
wrote me a nineteen-page letter, in clear script and correct
English. It started with a hound that in his passion for killing rattlesnakes became immune to their poison, and proceeded to numerous characters and observations, all interesting. I quote one account.

"One day in the '30's while I was working for the Houston Pipe Line Company at Mount Lucas in Live Oak
County, some of us went to Skidmore to work on a regula-
tor station. This station was close to the highway, on the
edge of town. About three o'clock in the afternoon the foreman and I noticed a man walking along the shoulder of the
road, carrying a small suitcase in one hand and a canvas-
covered object on his back. The object appeared to be a
box, about eighteen inches long and maybe ten inches
wide and as many deep. The man was of medium build,
plainly but cleanly dressed.

"We were not very busy at the moment, and as the man neared us, I could see that the foreman, who was always curious, itched to find out what that canvas-covered box held. There was nothing to indicate that it held anything besides clothes and other personal possessions, but the foreman could not sit still. He stepped out to the road and asked the man where he was going. He was going to Beeville, he said. The foreman told him that if he would wait a while we would take him in our car, as we were going that way also.

"The stranger came over to where we were. He put his suitcase on the ground, but kept the canvas-covered box on his back. He stood there without making any move to rest himself from the burden. Meanwhile the foreman's curiosity rose to just about the boiling point. After several hints and allusions to the box that brought no information, the foreman asked flatly what was in it.

"The stranger did not answer a word. He took the straps that held the box off his shoulders and set it on the ground. Then he raised the lid. All we could see was a tow sack. Without pulling it from the box, he untwisted one end, ran his hand down into it, felt around, and came out with a rattlesnake about three and a half feet long. He had it grasped just back of the head and he held it out almost into the foreman's face. That seemed to satisfy the foreman's curiosity, but the stranger's reticence was now broken.

"He told how he caught and sold snakes for a livelihood. No, he said, he was not scared of being bitten, for he had become virtually immune to rattlesnake poison. He put the rattler back in the tow sack and then showed us twenty-two places on his hands where rattlesnake fangs had gone in. Each place was marked by two narrow scars about half an inch long from slits he had made through the fang punctures with a razor blade. He said that slitting the wound and applying a tourniquet to keep the poison from circulating were his only remedies. Gradually he had built up an immunity to the poison, so that now when a snake bit him he paid little attention to it.

"He got out of our car at Beeville, strapped the canvas-covered box onto his back and walked away. I have never heard of him since."

This fellow was very different in showmanship from Billy Anderson of the Jack Hays Texas Rangers in the Mexican War. I met him in a curious book entitled *Chile con Carne*, by S. Compton Smith, who was a surgeon with General Taylor's army in Mexico. One day, the surgeon wrote, as he approached the Ranger camp, he noticed a group of Texians under the shade of a large tree highly interested in something. Riding over to the group, he saw "an old man" — probably in his thirties — seated on a log and holding a wicker cage that contained a large, angrily buzzing rattlesnake.

This was Billy Anderson. He was on one of his sprees. For a drink of whiskey he would grasp the snake by the neck, just back of the jaws, draw it forth from the cage, and present the back of his left hand or the upper portion of his arm for the snake to sink its fangs into. There was no doubt about the snake's being venomous. It sank its fangs, now, into Billy Anderson's arm. The arm and hand were covered with scars from former bites.

Billy Anderson carried a pocketful of small roots from one of the weeds called the rattlesnake's master. He chewed some of the roots, swallowed the juice and applied the pulp to the bite. He followed the rule, however, of never allowing a snake to bite him while he was sober, for, he said, "the rattlesnake's master is not always sure without the whiskey."

Billy Anderson brings up another "curiosity of a man," named Clark Stanley. In 1897 he published at Providence, Rhode Island, a thickish pamphlet entitled *The Life and Adventures of the American Cowboy, by Clark Stanley, Better Known as the Rattle Snake King*. A good part of the pamphlet is taken up with praises for Clark Stanley's Snake Oil Liniment. According to the author, he had been a cowboy in Texas during the 1870's, had drifted west and taken up with the Hopi Indians, famous for their annual snake dance to bring rain, and had learned from Hopi medicine men "the secret of snake oil." Clark Stanley had been bitten hundreds of times by rattlesnakes. He publishes the testimony of others as to the many scars from snakebites on his body. But he was not immune. He always used a remedy, an absolute and guaranteed remedy, the formula for which had been given him by the Hopi Indians. There was no alcohol in this remedy, but I still think Governor O. M. Roberts of Texas was right when he asked, "Who would want a better remedy than whiskey?"

A Dissertation on Lying About Snakes

SOME PEOPLE LIE for money, whether pocket change or millions; some lie for office, peanut jobs and on up. The most fashionable form of lying among politicians nowadays is the assumption of piety, the liars exhibiting — by words only — self-holiness. When Charles Lamb said, "I am a matter-of-lie kind of man," he was merely expressing irritation at the dull stuffed shirts always setting themselves up as matter-of-fact people. Liars who lie for fun can be engaging.

Some lies about snakes are generated out of ignorance; some out of a wish to please. People were lying about snakes long before any alphabet was invented. Eve had already eaten the forbidden fruit when she tried to lay the blame on a snake.

Many years ago an ancient Negro man working in our yard distinguished himself by trying to kill every lizard he saw. I asked him why he wanted to kill them. He said that if one ran down his throat he (the man) would die. I asked him how one would get down his throat. He didn't know. A similar story from Greece is probably thousands of years old. A man fell asleep under a fig tree with his mouth open, and a snake crawled down his throat. When he awoke he called some relatives and told them what had happened. Don't ask me how he knew. Nobody knew what to do for him or for the snake until a wise man came along. He sent a woman to a house not far off to bring a saucer of warm milk. Then he got the man who had been asleep to turn over on his stomach and hold his mouth open right over the saucer of milk. As soon as the snake smelled the milk, he crawled out of the man's stomach and began lapping it. Neither man nor snake had been injured by the gargantuan excursion.

When the great naturalist Audubon wrote an article in which he described a rattlesnake chasing a squirrel up one tree, down another, and across the topmost branches as well as on the ground of a forested area, he raised a furious argument that has not been altogether settled to this day. Had he described the squirrel as being so "charmed" by a rattlesnake that it allowed the snake to swallow it before it was dead, the argument would have been just as fierce and prolonged.

In Jean Bernard Bossu's *Travels in the Interior of North America, 1751-1762*, translated and edited by Seymour Feiler and published by the University of Oklahoma Press, there is the following instance of what the traveler says he experienced:

"I have often heard Frenchmen and Indians say that snakes have the ability to fascinate or charm squirrels. One day I was hunting in Illinois country, where there is a great quantity of hazelnuts. There were also many squirrels, since they are particularly fond of these nuts.

"I suddenly heard a squirrel, in a tree under which I was standing, make a pitiful noise, as though it were frightened. I did not know what was wrong with the animal until I saw a snake hanging from a branch of the tree. It held its head raised and waited for its prey. After having jumped from branch to branch, the poor squirrel fell into the snake's mouth and was swallowed.

"Without going into great detail, I believe that this is how the squirrel was hypnotized by the snake. The squirrel, which has a natural aversion to the snake, seeing its enemy hanging motionless from a branch, thinks that it is caught in the tree. Not realizing that this is just a trap, the squirrel jumps from branch to branch as though to mock the snake in its trouble. When the animal jumps too close, the snake darts forward, seizes its prey, and swallows it."

And this takes us to gaucho talk in W. H. Hudson's *The Purple Land* — a book not nearly so well known as his *Green Mansions* but more congenial to me. The talk is around the evening campfire out on the pampas.

" 'The manner in which the lampalagua captures its prey is very curious,' said one of the company, named Rivarola, a stout man with an immense fierce-looking black beard and moustache, but who was very mild-eyed and had a gentle, cooing voice.

"We had all heard of the lampalagua, a species of boa

found in these countries, with a very thick body and extremely sluggish in its motions. It preys on the larger rodents, and captures them, I believe, by following them into their burrows, where they cannot escape from its jaws by running.

" 'I will tell you what I once witnessed," continued Rivarola. 'Riding one day through a forest I saw some distance before me a fox sitting on the grass watching my approach. Suddenly I saw it spring high up into the air, uttering a great scream of terror, then fall back upon the earth, where it lay for some time growling, struggling, and biting as if engaged in deadly conflict with some invisible enemy. Presently it began to move away through the wood, but very slowly and still frantically struggling. It seemed to be getting exhausted, its tail dragged, the mouth foamed, and the tongue hung out, while it still moved on as if drawn by an unseen cord.

" 'I followed, going very close to it, but it took no notice of me. Sometimes it dug its claws into the ground or seized a twig or stalk with its teeth, and it would then remain resting for a few moments till the twig gave away, when it would roll over many times on the ground, loudly yelping, but still dragged onwards. Presently I saw in the direction we were going a huge serpent, thick as a man's thigh, its head lifted high above the grass, and motionless as a serpent of stone. Its cavernous, blood-red mouth was gaping wide, and its eyes were fixed on the struggling fox. When about twenty yards from the serpent, the fox began moving very rapidly over the ground, its struggles growing feebler every moment, until it seemed to fly through the air, and in an instant was in the serpent's mouth. Then the reptile dropped its head and began slowly swallowing its prey.'

" 'And you actually witnessed this yourself?' said I.

" 'With these eyes,' he returned, pointing at them with the tube of the maté-cup he held in his hand. 'This was the only one occasion on which I have actually seen the lampalagua take its prey, but its manner of doing it is well known to everyone from hearsay. You see, it draws an animal towards it by means of its power of suction. Sometimes, when the animal attacked is very strong or very far off — say two thousand yards — the serpent becomes so inflated with the quantity of air inhaled while drawing the victim towards it —'

" 'That it bursts?' I suggested.

" 'That it is obliged to stop drawing, to blow the wind out. When this happens, the animal, finding itself released from the drawing force, instantly sets off at full speed. Vain effort! The serpent has no sooner discharged the accumulated wind with a report like a cannon —'

" 'No, no, like a musket! I have heard it myself,' interrupted Blas Aria, one of the listeners.

" 'Like a musket, than it once more brings its power of suction to bear; and in this manner the contest continues until the victim is finally drawn into the monster's jaws. It is well known that the lampalagua is the strongest of all

God's creatures, and that if a man, stripped to the skin, engages one, and conquers it by sheer muscular strength, the serpent's power goes into him, after which he is invincible.'

"I laughed at this fable, and was severely rebuked for my levity."

If the word "charm" is interdicted by science, one may at least say that the rattlesnake at times exerts a horrible influence upon man as well as upon animals. That the human beings so affected are possessed of an unusual imagination does not disprove the theory of snake fascination.

C. B. Ruggles described to me an experience he had as a child. While he was hunting sheep sorrel one day, wandering ahead of some other children, he became conscious of a rattlesnake not more than three feet in front of him. The snake was not rattling but was swaying its head very slowly and gently. Ruggles felt sick. He was on his hands and knees, and only by stiffening his arms and exerting great willpower could he resist the tendency to go forward. Some of the other children saw him and thought he was "funny." One of them kicked him. At the kick his head dropped, and, thus "released" from the snake's gaze, he backed away. He was so sick that he vomited while his companions stoned the snake to death.

Years after he was a grown man Ruggles observed a blackbird that was on a limb only a few feet from the ground acting in a most peculiar manner. Its feathers were disheveled, its wings drooping, and its claws clutching a twig as if in agonized desperation. Looking about, Ruggles saw a noiseless rattler in the grass below the bird swaying its head. He had a six-shooter, and, needless to say, he shot the head off.

A Mexican whom I have known all my life and would trust with everything I have told me how a rattlesnake once *almost* charmed him. He saw it in a thicket and dismounted from his horse to kill it. Approaching it from the front, he got a glare of its eyes. Never before had he been afraid of rattlesnakes, and he had killed hundreds of them. But now, all at once, he felt the ligaments of his knees give way, and he nearly fell to the earth. His bones seemed to be collapsing in the joints. He was so weak that he could not lift a stick he held in his hand to strike the snake. But, after it had "sung" and threatened for a while, the snake glided away, leaving the Mexican to recover.

In Borden County, Joseph J. Good once saw, near his brother's corral, a rabbit jumping about in a peculiar manner and upon investigation discovered that it was hypnotized — paralyzed with fear — by a large rattlesnake. The rabbit seemed powerless to run off. It would jump up and then, seeming fascinated, move within striking distance of the rattlesnake. He saw the rattler strike the rabbit "a half dozen times" before he took a hand and killed it. I have heard eyewitness accounts of rabbits being "charmed" by rattlesnakes, but this is the only instance I have heard of

[83]

a rattler's finding it necessary to strike its prey more than once in order to kill it. A rattlesnake does not usually waste its ammunition.

One pioneer has left it on record that he once saw a rattlesnake charming a bird by means of its tongue, "one fork of it darkish, the other reddish or yellow, both of them gently moving like worms" to decoy the bird. Equally absurd is the claim of the Modoc Indians that the frog can resist being charmed because he is able to swell up. I myself have seen a frog so paralyzed with fear that it could not hop while a common rat snake approached and seized it.

Nor can I altogether accept the story of the Arkansas yarb-woman already alluded to. She knew a family that became much puzzled by the actions of one of the children, a little girl. The child appeared to have normal health, yet was visibly pining away. After a while the parents observed that although she took food, she was not eating it at the table but would slip away with it in her hand. The fare was very simple, mostly bread and potatoes. One day when the little girl left the table, her father followed her. He saw her slip into some bushes back of the woodpile, and there he beheld a sight that almost froze his blood. Noiselessly approaching the child, its head reared high, and its tongue gently moving back and forth as if in anticipation of its daily ration, was an enormous rattlesnake. It was in the very act of taking the bread from his daughter's hand when the father leaped forth and with a stick of wood killed it. The child went into a passion of tears. She had been starving herself to feed her fatal charmer; now she did nothing but grieve, and within a few weeks she died.

While I have never been charmed by a rattlesnake, I have in the presence of one had sensations that make me believe the reactions of certain other people under similar conditions might approach paralysis. On one occasion I was stalking a deer when I heard the low warning rattle of the terror of all hunters in the Southwest. I looked, and there on the bank of a shallow gully that I was following lay coiled the largest rattler I have ever met. I could smell him. His scales were rusty and coarse. The hair of my head began to rise; cold shivers ran down my back; the entire surface of my body became gooseflesh. I was not within striking distance of the rattlesnake, and so, I suppose, I did not have fear. I looked about for a stick or rock of some kind with which to kill the snake. The only plant growth within sight was switch mesquite and low chaparral. There were no rocks; the soil afforded not even a clod. If I shot, I should ruin my chances of approaching the buck, which was yet out of range. But now the deer was nothing. I was filled with hatred for the horrid reptile whose presence rather than threat enraged me. I understood well how primordial man regarded the snake as symbolic of all evil, though I wonder that such a regard should have arisen among people who did not know the rattlesnake. I aimed my thirty-thirty and killed the monster. He measured over six feet. Two other times I have in the presence of a particularly large and vicious rattlesnake experienced the same overwhelming sensations.

Rattlesnakes and an Inferiority Complex

As TOLD TO ME by Judge J. R. Wilhelm of San Marcos, Texas, there used to live on the Blanco River in Hays County, Texas, a family by the name of Dickens. The head of the family was a great deer hunter, but he got enough brush cleared off his five hundred acres of land to plant a patch of corn and was thriving until he built a house. Moving into it upset him. He simply could not bear the idea of being settled, and so he sold out and moved to Runnels County, where he found some good land, raised some good crops, and was in a way trapped into being settled and prosperous. However, this is not a story of the pioneer temperament.

While living in the hills along the Blanco River, the Dickens family became noted for being bitten by rattlesnakes. There were plenty of rattlers in the country, and one day while Mr. Dickens was crawling up on a buck, paying full attention to making no noise and to his target, a snake bit him in the wrist. He made a slash or two around the bite, sucked out the poisoned blood, and came home with venison. Next a snake bit Mrs. Dickens while she was cleaning up camp; it was cool weather, and the rattler had crawled into some bedding for warmth. She got all right.

Then Sambo, the oldest son, got bit while he and his brother Cottonhead were twisting a cottontail rabbit out of a hollow stump. The family ate lots of rabbit meat when venison was scarce. The dogs had chased this rabbit into the hollow stump, and without waiting to investigate, Sambo had reached in for it and received a sharp bite. The boys cut the rabbit open and laid the hot flesh to the bite, and Sambo got all right. Next Cottonhead and the other boy, Reuben, were bitten, and then Maria.

Finally Dolly, the youngest of the family, was the only one left unbitten. Any visitor who came was sure to be regaled with details of all the snakebites the members of the family had experienced. They expanded on the lengths of the snakes, on the number of rattles each had, and on the horrors of the poison. They had the clan spirit and were exceedingly proud of their record — all but Dolly. When the talk turned on rattlesnakes, she would hide behind her mother's skirt. "Rattlesnakes don't think enough of Dolly to even bite her," Mr. Dickens would tease, little knowing how the remark cut the girl to the quick. She would walk around barefooted in high weeds hoping to step on a rattlesnake and receive a good bite, but never a one could she rouse. She was timid at school, and the other children, echoing her father's teasing, made life miserable for her. She became the silent household drudge, hiding her misery in humility. It was a relief to her when the family put their goods in a wagon and, with the boys riding horseback and driving a few cows, set out west.

One July day out there while hoeing their first cotton crop, Sambo got bit again. "Well, the second round has started," Mr. Dickens said. "Maybe Dolly will have her chance yet. This is good snake country." All the new neighbors were learning the Dickens family record with rattlesnakes. Dolly's abashment was renewed and intensified. Facing other children at school was a daily agony. She was growing up now. She felt as marked as a child would feel at being the only one not getting a present off a beautiful Christmas tree. She was the white blackbird.

Then one evening while she was walking through broomweeds after the milk cows, a rattlesnake bit her. No maiden was ever more invigorated by a first kiss. Gladness in her eyes, joy in her voice, elation in every movement, she came running to the house, crying, "One bit me, one bit me, one bit me!" The bite was in the calf of her leg, and soaking it in a can of kerosene was the only remedy applied. The snake probably injected just a small amount of poison. Anyway, Dolly went to school next day a changed individual. No longer was she a pariah among the elected. She became the brightest and most eager scholar not only of her family but of the school. In time she received a certificate to teach school, the first of the Dickens family to advance that far in learning. She taught school successfully, and when the talk turned on rattlesnakes, she led it in proud recital of each bite that her father, her mother, her sister, her brothers and she herself had received. She would laugh at how long it took her to offend a rattlesnake. She married a well-to-do rancher and lived happy ever afterwards.

Smelling Rattlesnakes on the Front Gallery

THIS WIDE, LONG front gallery, the floor of which is only a few inches above the ground, is at Paisano. Paisano is not an estate, not a ranch, not a farm; it is merely a place of some acres in the hills west of Austin, Barton Creek winding through it, a high, rocky bluff on one side and then on the other side, alternating with meadows. The front gallery is provided with a couch, a cot, a bench, and a diversity of chairs. O. Henry's Sam Galloway, in the story called "The Last of the Troubadours," would have delighted in it. Sam never stood when he could sit, and he never sat when he could lie down. There I like to emulate Sam Galloway, listening, if the wind isn't too high, to the water over the riffles in the creek just down a slope, gazing at faraway hills and especially at a patch of waving blue-stem grass. It's a fine place from which to look at the clouds lazing along from the south, and at the variety of green on Spanish oaks, live oaks, pecans, elms, sycamores and other trees. It's a fine place in the evening to receive a visit from a hognosed skunk. Lingering there, one can nearly always delight in the gracefulness of a buzzard in the air; in the summer scissortails, vermilion flycatchers, chimney swifts and other feeders upon airborne insects add to the charm of life.

After I published among some of my encounters with particular rattlesnakes a story about a big one that I smelled before I saw him, a number of people conversed by letter with me on the subject. I've invited some of them to the Paisano front gallery. Of course, our talk meanders. To save space, I'll introduce each converser, let him have his say on the subject — and nothing else.

Here is Mrs. Daisy R. Binkley of Austin. Back in the '30's she was living at an outpost called Rancho Viejo on the big Callahan ranch in Webb County. Not far to the rear of the house was a dirt tank in which the manager's son had turned loose a small alligator. It grew to be six feet long.

"One fine day in May," to quote Mrs. Binkley, "I went down to this tank to see if I could glimpse the alligator. Rattlesnakes were out of my mind while I scanned the opposite bank for the alligator. All of a sudden I smelled something different, sort of like a wasp when it is hot and mad. I dropped my eyes to the ground in front of me and saw an enormous rattler stretched across the bare ground of the tank dam, about five feet off. I got away like an old javelina sow with piglets. I was too shook up to hunt for anything to kill the snake with. As far as I know it stayed on where it was and snoozed. I've been near small rattlers when they were killed, but this is the only rattler I ever smelled. It's my belief that if I had not smelled it I would have walked right on up to the snake."

I'm looking for somebody with a keen nose to detect the smell of a hot, mad wasp.

Allow me to introduce now another Austin citizen, William O. George, geologist. He has geologized in Mexico and other Spanish countries to the south. "When I was young," he says, "on my first work in Mexico, I took the lead with my machete, cutting paths through the jungle. I learned better than that. By the time I reached Colombia to make a survey for an oil company four hundred miles up the Magdalena River, I kept to the rear of a crew of six or eight men cutting senderos. The foreman was one of those persons who can smell snakes. From time to time he would stop, lift his head, wrinkle his nose and shout, 'Víbora!' This meant that he smelled a boa constrictor. At the warning every man in the machete crew would freeze and look about until one saw the boa constrictor and chopped his head off with a deft swish. I myself have never smelled a snake of any kind, and none of the other men of this crew seemed gifted with a snake-smelling nose. The boa constrictors we encountered were from ten to twelve feet long, and most of them seemed to be asleep. In that jungle we didn't have a chance at rattlesnakes, but any man who could smell a boa constrictor should be able to smell a rattler."

W. C. Bricker is a constable out at Sonora and a positive man, as a constable had better be sometimes. These are his words:

"My wife had gotten into the habit of taking garbage to the garbage can after dark, about fifty yards from the house. I warned her that she'd better take a flashlight and watch out for snakes. Generally she paid no attention to my advice. One night after supper she went out as usual without a light and soon I heard her scream. She wasn't far behind the sound in getting to the house. She had run into Mr. Rattler. I grabbed the shotgun but couldn't find a flashlight, and so headed out without it. I could hear the snake though. He was buzzing and crawling up a fairly steep grade through short grass and weeds and rolling small rocks or pebbles down. I knew from the noise that it was a good-sized rattler. Then I smelled a peculiar odor. It was as distinct as the odor from a decaying human body. The snake when I killed him shortly afterwards measured four and one-half feet long and was thick through. Until you wrote of smelling a rattlesnake, I never mentioned to anybody that I smelled this rattler in the night. I didn't want to be taken for a liar, but will swear to what I've said."

My butcher friend Doc Polk raises quarter horses on the edge of Austin. His eyes have the look of having gazed far away in a land of distances and intense light. He sits quiet on a rawhide chair here on the gallery. He's looking far away and listening. Then he joins in by mentioning three quarter horses he used to ride on a ranch in broken country where Scurry, Kent, Stonewall and Fisher counties corner. There were and still are lots of rattlesnakes in the breaks of that country. Each of these three horses would on occasion point his ears in a certain direction. Doc Polk would pay attention and learned that the horse was pointing towards a rattlesnake he'd smelled out.

I would suppose that rattlesnakes lying in wait for rodents, their main prey, either take advantage of the wind, like a panther stalking a colt, or are odorless for the time being like a wild turkey sitting on her nest. Has anybody studied snakes closely enough to be sure on the subject?

Dean of all the rattlesnake-smellers here on the Paisano front gallery, as well as elsewhere, is Charles Deaton of Dumont, Texas. He does not define "authority," but says that an authority once estimated that there were three thousand snakes in Rattlesnake Bend on the Brazos River in Stonewall County. Rattlesnake Bend consists of five or six acres of gyp formation, honeycombed with caves.

"One Sunday," said Mr. Deaton, "I took two boys with me, each of us armed with a .22 Winchester, to shoot snakes. We had at least five hundred shells. Half a mile before we came to the head of the draw that sinks into the caves of Rattlesnake Bend we all smelled a heavy, musky kind of scent. Our ammunition was all gone before we got half around the gyp sink. In 1905 I bought a tract of land from the H. & T. C. Railroad Company between the Brazos and Stinking Creek. I lived here for seventeen years and visited Rattlesnake Bend many times. That musty scent always came into my nostrils before I got to the cave. When oil was found close to the bend someone took nitroglycerin and blew up the great rattlesnake hibernating place."

Cat and Rattlesnake

ONE OF THE MOST OBSERVANT, alert-minded and interesting recounters of his observations ever to pursue knowledge in Texas was H. B. Parks of the Texas State Apicultural Research Laboratory near San Antonio. His writings have been published in bee journals, by the Texas Academy of Science, the Texas Folklore Society and elsewhere, but I am pretty sure that some of his best things have not been published at all. He was a scientist who was also eager about all things human. A good many years ago now, he gave me the following narrative, written June 29, 1928, not long after the cat died.

The cat was a female of about normal size. She was of no special variety. In color she was black and white spotted. Her origin was unknown. At the time she appeared at the Laboratory she must have been of considerable age as her front teeth were missing. She lived at the Apicultural Laboratory for four and a half years and was the progenitor of forty-two known descendants and probably of some unknown. We called her Momsie Cat.

She was a hunter from the very beginning, and preferred to catch her own food and that of her kittens rather than take scraps from the house. She never would eat anything she caught without first bringing it to some member of the family at the Laboratory. Thus we had a definite knowledge of what she ate. She was not strong enough to carry a full-grown jackrabbit, but she quite often brought full-grown ones to the Laboratory by walking backward and dragging the carcass.

The Laboratory is located between the black mesquite lands east of San Antonio and the sandy post-oak lands. Annually, from about October 15 until spring, this country is inhabited by a large number of migratory birds, and during this period the cat had no trouble whatever in catching more birds than she and her family could eat. From March to October 15 there are very few birds and these are so wild that the cat seemingly could not catch them. Rodents and other small animals are extremely scarce. So, for more than six months of the year, the cat was almost forced to another source of food. During this period her diet consisted largely of various varieties of snakes, lizards, horned toads, grasshoppers, and beetles. Not only the mother cat but also her successive litters of kittens ate snakes, lizards and the like with a great deal of pleasure. The kittens seemed to like grasshoppers better than any other summer food.

The first rattlesnake we saw in the possession of the cat was only about two and a half feet long. While we did not see her kill it, it was still moving when she brought it to the house. A short time afterward she brought in a little rattlesnake about eleven inches long that had been dead for some considerable time. In August, 1924, a man employed by the Laboratory to do manual labor came to the office and asked if we would like to see Momsie Cat kill a rattlesnake.

The entire office force followed him, and on a piece of flat ground not very far from the Laboratory building we saw the mother cat with three half-grown kittens in battle with a rattlesnake approximately four feet long. The laboring man said that his wife had heard a rattlesnake making a great deal of noise near their house and on looking out of the door saw the cat watching the rattlesnake. She called her husband, and he saw the battle from the beginning. He said that the cat waited till the rattlesnake was coiled before making a spring towards it. When the rattlesnake struck, the cat dodged the blow; then, as the rattlesnake stretched itself out while striking, the cat would bite at the back of its neck.

At the time we were called, the rattlesnake lay stretched out on the road and was rattling rather feebly while attempting to crawl into some brush. The old cat would walk up slowly until she was about a foot from the rattlesnake's head and would then suddenly jump on the snake's back, bite its neck, and run. She repeated this action a number of times. Each attack left the snake in a weaker condition, and at last he coiled up and ceased to rattle. Finally, the old cat approached cautiously and, catching him by the back of the neck, started to drag him towards the house. When she became conscious that she was being watched, she left the rattlesnake and came over to where we stood. She appeared to be exhausted by the fight she had had. On examination, the back of the snake's head was found to be full of punctures from her teeth.

This cat was very active as a hunter up to about six months before her death, when she lost the last tooth out of her jaws and thenceforth had to be fed on soft foods supplied by the household. The diet did not seem to nourish her. She died in 1927 in a fit, perhaps brought on by starvation.

The Way of a Boy and a Girl
with Rattlesnakes

IN RELATING in my newspaper column some of my own experiences with rattlesnakes I invited experiences from others on the subject. They came in — along with a strong protest from an old-time friend against my having any more to say about rattlesnakes.

I feel as if I were only a kind of director of conversation on a given subject. The majority will have to rule for a little while. Edgar Allan Poe laid down as the primary law of the short story that nothing should go into it that does not contribute to "the inevitable end." I like the lingering way that people have in narrating personal experiences. The end is seldom inevitable.

The following is from Mrs. Sam J. Gore of Austin, Texas. She concludes her letter by saying that if any child of her own decided to hunt snakes for spending money, she would brain it.

In 1931 money was as tight as Dick's hatband. I was twelve and my brother sixteen. We were beginning to realize the value of money, mostly through the lack of it. Mother often let us have the eggs to sell, at twelve cents a dozen, the top price. One day we sold our eggs for enough money to stay in town and see a tent show. What a wonderful thrill that was — but we knew those hens would never lay enough eggs during the next few days for us to see the show again. While we were riding home very quietly in the dark, a possum ran into the road just ahead of us. The brakes of the old T-model Ford screeched, and I immediately got in Billie's way. He grabbed the crank and was out of the car before it stopped rolling. He chased that possum down, applied the crank, and was back in the car before I could yell encouragement. The next evening we went to town, this time with a fresh possum hide. We sold it and had plenty to see the show.

Trapping became our winter recreation, occupation, and sole source of money. While Billie worked hard at it, he learned of a market for snakes, especially rattlesnakes. As the spring days warmed up, he watched eagerly. When he found our first big rattler, he unlaced his shoe, found a nice long stick, tied his shoestring to the stick and made a loop in the other end of it. By punching at the snake he made it raise its head as though to strike; then he raised the stick and slipped the noose over the snake's head and tightened up. All he had to do now was to drag the snake home and face Mother. Our home was on the Albert Pfluger ranch west of Round Rock. It had over a thousand acres in it, and I guess about that many snakes per acre.

We needed a place to keep all these snakes we planned on catching and decided on some old metal oil drums that had the tops cut out. Mother wouldn't allow them any closer than behind the garage. We snared one rattler so large that it could rear up and almost get out of the barrel. We finally had to put a lid on that one, but we left the others open.

My mother was a nervous wreck by this time. She hated to go to see the neighbors or even to town to get groceries because she knew the minute she was out of sight the hunt would be on! She knew there was always that chance of a slip-up, though we never gave it a thought. Shoestrings were cheap and rattlers were forty-five cents per pound, and the Old Settlers Reunion at Round Rock, with its carnival, was soon to start. We needed all the snakes we could round up. We sold our snakes to the sideshow at the carnival and had a wonderful time for a week.

We had lost only one. It was in a barrel with several other snakes and one of them must have gotten hungry. Another snake was caught too late to sell, so we just kept her. We became attached to her and moved her barrel into the yard under the trees where she would be cool. We visited her every day and often dropped pieces of hamburger to her. I never saw her eat them, but they were always gone at our next visit. Mother was glad when the mornings began to get so cool that we complained of our snake's being stiff. She convinced Dad that the human thing to do was for him to kill our snake. He waited until we had gone to school and went to the barrel fully intending to commit murder. He took one look and called for Mother. She knew he had been bitten, and she couldn't drive the car; she knew he would be dead before she could get help; she hated herself for asking him to kill that snake.

When she got outside she saw Dad looking into the barrel with deep admiration. "Look, Norma," he said, "she's had pups!" Sure enough, there were nine little rattlers, pale gray, pink-nosed, black-tongued, each with a trace of a button on the end of the tail. We were so happy for the matriarch that Dad let us keep the whole family until her children were larger than new pencils. Every few days we lowered a fruit jar lid with milk and egg into the barrel and it was always gone on our next visit. The old snake never seemed to mind our visits. Dad finally killed them all when the weather got too cold for them. It was hard for us to let him do it, but we couldn't keep them any longer. We did find that rattlers have an odor when calm and a different odor when mad. The odor from the venom will also make you nauseated if you get a good breath of it.

With Friendly Feelings for Rattlesnakes

IN MARCH, 1944, while I was across the Atlantic, Lee Lewis, then of Laredo, wrote me a letter, in order to tell a story. It is about the only pet of its kind I know. Lee Lewis got it from a man named Odom, then about seventy years old, who ran Odom's Sandwich Stand in Laredo.

In his young days Odom cowboyed in northwest Texas for C. C. Slaughter, whose Long S brand was worn by tens of thousands of cattle on ranches in Texas, Wyoming and Montana. Odom worked for him on a ranch of one hundred and forty sections leased from the state of Texas. In winter the cattle were taken care of from eleven outposts, each with a well-equipped cabin and one man. Odom kept two old saddle horses on feed. One was always under saddle or within sight of the cabin.

One evening his horses coming in for feed were accompanied by a young Angora billygoat. So far as Odom knew, there were no goats in the country nearer than seventy-five miles from his cabin. The goat and the horses became inseparable.

Spring came and with the first warm sunshine a rattlesnake three or four feet long showed up near the cabin. Odom had been pleased at the addition of the billygoat's company, and now he did not disturb the snake. It got to where it would crawl out from under the house between Odom's feet while he sat on the porch with his feet on the ground. He would sit still and let it crawl around. Before long the snake would allow him to walk around it and even to step over it, quietly. Before the snake showed up, wood-rats and skunks under the cabin floor often disturbed Odom at all hours of the night, but never thereafter. He didn't know whether the snake was male or female; he named it Long S.

Long S was a playful snake. It would crawl up near the old horse's right hind leg and coil as if to strike and even pretend to strike. When the horse kicked at it, the rattler would throw itself out of the way. Eventually the horse would turn around and pretend to paw the snake, and the snake would keep on playing at striking and shying out of reach of the hoofs.

Long S and the goat used to play likewise. The snake would crawl out to where the goat was in the open; then the goat would rear up on his hind legs and pretend to crush it with his front hoofs.

"Did the snake ever rattle when playing with the horse or the goat?"

"Never," Odom answered.

"What happened to the snake?"

Odom filed on four sections of state land surrounding

the cabin and added another room for his bride to move into. Shortly after the marriage he was summoned to court more than a day's ride away. Before leaving, he got the young daughter (Pearl Fish, ten years old) of his nearest neighbor, eighteen miles away, to stay with his wife. He left his wife his six-shooter for protection, having taught her to fire it. When he got back home, the first thing she told him was that she had shot an awful big rattlesnake right there in front of the house. He hadn't taught her not to shoot his pets. The news left him speechless.

The other day Mr. W. F. Hutson, a retired surveyor of Austin, gave me these anecdotes on friendly feelings towards rattlesnakes.

One time while he was surveying in Kinney County, between Brackettville and Spofford, a man who was walking with him across a dry creek yelled like bloody murder for him to jump. He jumped but didn't know why until he looked back and saw a big rattlesnake. The snake was lying quiet beside the trail. When the other man grabbed for a rock or a stick to kill it Hutson objected. "This snake didn't do anything to me," Hutson said, "and I'm not going to do anything to him. He didn't want to hurt me. He just tended to his own business."

A chuck wagon cook in Edwards County told Hutson he never would kill a rattlesnake. His explanation was something like this: One night while his outfit was camped near the Devil's Sink Hole, a pit famous for bats, cave swallows and depth, he stepped away to rustle for wood. He got out of sight of the chuck wagon and lantern and was carrying an armful of wood along in the right direction, as he thought, when just in front of him he heard a violent whirring of rattles. He threw his wood down right there and took off in another direction. He found the chuck wagon. Next morning after the cow crowd rode off, he had a little time. He was curious about how he'd lost his direction the night before. He looked around and found the armful of wood he'd thrown down — at the very edge of the Devil's Sink Hole. If that rattlesnake hadn't rattled he would have stepped into the hole and gone down a hundred feet or so, breaking his neck and all other bones for sure. After that he would not, under any circumstances, kill a rattlesnake. One of the species had saved his life, and he wasn't going to take the life of a single individual belonging to the species.

Rover the Rattlesnake Dog

FOR THE FOLLOWING first-hand observations on rattle-snakes and experiences with them, we are all indebted to John C. Myers of Eagle Pass, Texas. The "I" and the "we" in the narrative belong to John C. Myers, here quoted without quotation marks.

Old Rover was hot on the trail of a coyote dragging a steel trap. My brother Clyde and I were right behind him. At first the trail was rather hard to follow, but soon went up a dry arroyo where we began to gain on the coyote. After a half-mile or so, he left the arroyo for an open grassy country, and Rover had to slow down somewhat. Finally he lost the trail altogether, in sandy loam country where "polecat" flowers (wild lantana) flourished, near a live oak motte.

Rover seemed to have trouble separating the scent of the coyote from that of the shrubby "polecat" flowers. He was sniffing and snuffing among the bushes. We were about ten feet away from him and were looking straight at him when he thrust his head into a certain clump.

Suddenly he backed up, and a large rattler that had struck him on the bony part of his muzzle, about halfway between nose and eyes, thrust itself into full view. Rover stood there momentarily in utter surprise, eying the rattler, which had assumed a striking position out in the open. Then Rover threw out the strangest roar I ever heard a dog give. He was in a fury over having been struck and charged straight at that rattlesnake, grabbing it viciously and shaking it with such ferocity that pieces of snake flew in all directions.

This happening was in Wilson County, Texas. I cannot say what part of the snake's body Rover grabbed. Many years have passed since then, but as I write now I see Rover in the center of fantastically fast action, his ears flapping, growls coming from his chest, his head a blur of motion, making of snake coils another blur. I do not think that Rover *bit* the snake in two. Reptiles are put together rather loosely and it takes no great effort to literally shake one to pieces.

Before long Rover held only a short piece of rattlesnake in his mouth. He dropped that and began to paw his nose and rub it vigorously in a clump of "polecat" flowers. He wallowed in dirt, shook himself vigorously and began hunting again. About a hundred yards out, we cut the trail and from there on it was easy to follow. About a mile farther on, we caught up with the coyote, which had snagged the trap in a hog-wire fence it had attempted to climb over. I was carrying a brand-new, single-shot, rim-fire, long-rifled, octagon-barreled Stevens Special .25 caliber rifle. Mr. Coyote was soon placed where he could catch no more of Mama's turkeys, which was the reason we were trapping for him.

We were about three miles from home, and now struck out for it at a trot, Rover leading the way. He stayed in the lead all the way, not once hunting out or paying attention to anything else but the beeline he was following. I shot a cottontail rabbit and tried to give it to Rover, but he would have none of it, which was most unusual behavior. He trotted past the peanut-stack lot, where he loved to lie and eat peanuts. He headed straight for his box, under the workbench in a shed just behind the smokehouse. Later on, we tried to feed him some table scraps, but he would not eat. Nor would he eat the next day or the next. He never left his box during this time, as far as we knew. His muzzle swelled some, but not excessively. However, the swelling around his eyes almost blinded him. A day or so later, I placed a pan of separated milk before him, and he eagerly lapped this up. He went back to his box, but later in the day he came out and lay in the sunshine. From that day on, his recovery was rapid and complete.

As long as he lived, Rover became an implacable and deadly hunter of rattlesnakes. Day and night, he "treed" rattlesnakes. We could always tell when he had located a snake, for on such an encounter he gave out a most weird, uncanny and unearthly howl. When we heard this, we grabbed hoe, pitchfork or rifle and went to his aid, for

Rover would stay with his rattlesnake until someone came. As far as we knew, he never attacked or killed another rattlesnake after the one had bitten him, although a small one he was baying struck him on the tip of his nose.

I never saw a house cat attack a rattlesnake, but cats do most of their hunting and prowling at night, out of sight. However, one day we noticed that our Chicken-House Cat, so called because she always slept on the roost with the hens, did not come out of the chicken house. Someone gathering the eggs that evening found the cat in a hen's nest. She appeared to be very sick, and her head was badly swollen. The next afternoon she was still on the nest, her head horribly swollen. The eyes were mere slits, she was completely blind, and she appeared to be in considerable pain. She never left the nest, as far as we knew, for a week. Finally she threw off the venom and recovered. But she was permanently marked; a scar ran diagonally from one ear to the tip of her nose. The skin had burst on this line from the pressure of pus.

Rattlesnakes in Waters Quiet
and Unquiet

ONLY TWICE IN MY LIFE have I seen rattlesnakes in
water. A good-sized one rested on a log floating
down the Colorado River on a big rise — before dams
above Austin came to control floodwaters. I judged that
this snake had already taken a considerable ride. The log
was out to one side of the main current, but so long as I
watched, it didn't lodge on a bank. The snake did not look
either alarmed or bored. It was just there, as a rock lies on
the ground or as fragments of cow chips left by receding
waters in a gully mark how high the waters have been.

My next sight was about 1920 in the Kintania pasture
of about twenty thousand acres in La Salle County, Texas
— a part of a big lease attached to the Olmos ranch then
owned by my Uncle Jim Dobie. A good portion of the Kintania is almost level black dirt and after rains little waterholes abound. As I rode up horseback to one of these little
waterholes, I saw two rattlesnakes swimming back and
forth, their tails held straight up out of the water. They
appeared to be swimming for fun, just as lots of other

people, including human beings, swim. I made some move that disturbed them, and before I could say "Scat" they disappeared in grass edging the water.

It used to be claimed that prairie dogs almost never made holes that floodwaters could reach, but that if they did make such holes, they would know when a flood was coming and desert for higher ground. I know that rattlesnakes care nothing for inhabiting land subject to overflow. I've killed many rattlesnakes in the sacahuiste that covers the Nueces River flats below Cotulla in La Salle County and is flooded when the Nueces gets on a fair rise.

Another big pasture attached to the Olmos ranch was the Wells, on down the Nueces River. John Barfield, who managed the Olmos early in this century, told me that one time while the Nueces was coming down on a rise he was in the Wells pasture and, riding along the edge of sacahuiste as the water came up into it, saw rattlesnakes moving out for dry ground. They were not scuttling on dry ground ahead of the water as animals flee a grass fire; most of them simply came out of the water. John Barfield had a six-shooter, and he said there were so many snakes that he used up all of his cartridges. Then he went to killing them with a doubled rope and got so tired getting down and lashing away that he finally just rode off and let the rattlesnakes come out free.

In September, 1937, the late Roy Bedichek, the most ample-natured naturalist of modern America, gave me these notes written down shortly after hearing E. E. Davis, of Arlington, talk. "Davis and his wife were in a motorboat on Lake Worth returning from a camping party. Davis, running the boat, saw ahead of him a snake swimming. He speeded up, intending to run it down, but on closer approach identified a huge rattler, swimming along at a leisurely pace with head well out of the water. The lake water was crystal clear; there could be no mistaken identity. Davis swerved the boat to one side, lest he throw the snake into it. He then circled the snake trying to hit it with an oar, but it threw itself into a coil to strike and bluffed Davis out, for he was afraid it might take a wrap on the oar and come right into the boat. The snake made for the shore and Davis circled it half a dozen times before it crawled up the bank, rattles vibrating. Davis saw them plainly but did not hear because of the roar of the motor in the boat.

"I have had hot arguments with old-timers in West Texas about the aquatic abilities of the rattler. I saw one swim a hole in Spring Creek near San Angelo when I was a boy. Davis gave me his account in the presence of his wife, who confirmed it. Here is an authentic case of a rattlesnake's ability not only to swim but to fight in the water."

Harold J. Cook, owner of the Agate Springs ranch in Nebraska, was a geologist with a disciplined mind. His father was James H. Cook, author of that interesting book *Fifty Years on the Old Frontier*. On February 12, 1955, Harold Cook wrote me in part as follows:

"One day I was trying to induce a large fat trout to take a hook I'd placed in a pool in our Niobrara River. He would play around with it but would not take hold. I was sitting on the ground near the edge of the stream in tall grass through which I could watch unobserved. After keeping still for some time, I became aware of a quiet rustling in the grass right beside me. Without moving my head, I glanced down and there, crawling through the grass slowly, within a few inches of my hip and leg, was a prairie rattler over three feet long. I had sat so long in one position that I was cramped and the snake was so close to me now that I didn't dare move. He glided slowly by and went into the stream. He swam across to the other side as easily as a water snake swims and disappeared into the tall grass. By the time I took my eye off him the trout was gone. In swimming, this rattlesnake held his rattles up an inch or so out of the water."

A scientist could not ask for more concrete evidence than was supplied to me by Paul Freier of Port Lavaca, Texas. I quote from his letter of June 20, 1960, as follows:

"Many people have seen many rattlesnakes floating or swimming in the waters of Lavaca Bay. Whether the snake floats in coiled position or swims in elongated position, the rattle is usually kept sticking up like a finger. Zane Dooley of Point Comfort, Texas, killed two rattlers with a gun from his boat in the middle of the bay on May 30, 1960. He reported to me that their rattles stuck up in the air and that they floated in the coiled position.

"Kerry Griffith of Francitas, Texas, reported to me that he observed a rattlesnake swimming across Pirates' Canal (upper Lavaca Bay) with his rattle out of the water in an upright position. When he threw a rock at the snake it ducked its rattle into the water and speeded up its swimming gait. My father and I watched a rattlesnake enter the water of Medio Creek (many years ago when it was a flowing stream in Refugio County), submerge completely, rattle and all, which was vigorously rattling, and emerge on the opposite bank, the rattle still flickering but without sound effects. This snake must have crawled across on the bottom of the stream bed as the armadillo is supposed to do, for we detected no sign of him on the surface or just beneath the surface.

"A common tradition is that the rattlesnake will not strike while in water. Robert Meyer and Ernest Kabela of Port Lavaca both reported to me that a rattlesnake they encountered in the middle of the bay with tail sticking up struck at an oar one of them struck at it while about three feet away. Both strikes were misses, but the snake struck the side of the boat at a greater distance than its own length. The snake fought very vigorously, neglecting to keep its rattles dry.

"Old Captain Frank Bauer, now deceased, of Port Lavaca always delighted in his tale of floating across Matagorda Bay on a heavy timber during the hurricane of 1887, which finished Indianola. He occupied one end of the timber and a rattlesnake the other. The snake seemed too preoccupied with keeping his rattle up to notice the man."

Mr. Paul Freier adds that people fishing with baited

hooks and also with rod and reel have dragged in rattle-snakes from shallow water. Snakes don't strike at a fly or at a baited hook, but if they are in the way when a hook is dragged over them, they are apt to get hung.

Between the Comanche and the
Rattlesnake

"GO AND CATCH a falling star," and I will tell you who, where, and when began the story of a man caught between the devil and the deep blue sea. According to a Buddhist fable, no doubt hoary before Buddha's advent in the sixth century before Christ, an enraged beast — some say a lion, some say a rhinoceros — was chasing a man across a plain when they came to a tree growing out of a wide and long-abandoned well. The man leaped to its branches and was safe from the beast, but, looking down, he saw a dragon at the bottom of the well. It was champing its jaws towards him in such fierce anger that fire blazed out of its eyes, mouth and nostrils.

The man grasped two branches of the tree, one in either hand, and planted his feet against the tree trunk at a kind of hump or knot. Then he saw four serpents darting out their heads from a hollow in the tree trunk right at his feet. He looked up and saw locusts, white and black, eating into the tree branches that he grasped so firmly. In time the branches were bound to fall. Then he noticed honey from a bee colony farther up the tree dripping on leaves within reach of his tongue. He licked the honey and found it sweet and forgot the raging beast at the edge of the well, the fiery dragon at the bottom, the threatening serpents at his feet, and the locusts cutting away his supports. "Now those who are dissolved in the seductive love of the world are like unto this man."

No moral is attached to any of the dilemmas of an American frontiersman shrinking between a rattlesnake about to strike on one hand and an Indian reaching for his scalp on the other. Varying stories that embody this dilemma are all told as fact. All come to the desperate situation without concern for rightness or wrongness, without one look into the Hamlet-deep well that every man covers up, without intimation of the complexities of human existence that are the stuff of literature. Repetition of violence and sensation divorced from those complexities wears them barren — and this may be a commentary on the mass of literature dealing with frontier life. Nevertheless, the repeated dilemmas between rattlesnake and scalper add up to a little saga. One might be tempted to call it the New World's Scylla and Charybdis, only no motive beyond that of a worm's instinct for life, no choice arising from his own dualities are given to the man fixed on the ground between Scylla-necked rattlesnake and Charybdisian vortex awaiting a scalpless skull.

The earliest of these dilemmas that I have encountered

was beyond the westernmost settlement of Virginia years before the American Revolution. I have been unable to establish the date, but the frontiersman involved, Charles Lewis, died about 1775. He came of desperate ancestry, his father having killed another landlord in Ireland, over property, before emigrating to America with family and tenants. He settled in western Virginia, where he and his sons became noted Indian fighters. Of all the family, Charles was the most noted. Physical bravery was — and is — a common virtue; Charles Lewis had, in addition to bravery, a quick wit, clear understanding, and a cool head.

One time while he was scouting alone ahead of a band of frontiersmen out to quell Indians, they ambushed him. He could kill one, but thought he might save his life by surrendering. The Indians took his hat, shoes, and most of his clothes, bound his arms behind him, and began driving and leading him to their own faraway camp. They abused him, but he bided his time. As the distance between them and possible rescuers increased, they became less vigilant, and one day while they were on the edge of a cliff overlooking a mountain torrent about twenty feet below, deep in woods and underbrush, he, by a violent effort, broke the cords binding his arms, and leaped.

Instantly he was out of sight, but yelling captors came hot behind. At one point one of them might have lanced him or shot an arrow into him, but their aim seemed to be to take him alive, and again he got out of sight. While he was leaping a long fallen tree in a dense thicket, he was tripped by briars and fell face to the ground on the other side. Already out of breath, he was for a short time unconscious. When he regained consciousness he heard his enemies close at hand and at the same time heard the muffled rattling of a rattlesnake that was coiled and reared "so near his face that its fangs were within a few inches of his nose."

If he moved, the movement could betray him to the Indians and also would probably make the rattler strike. If the Indians heard the rattling, would they not take it as a sign of an intruder, as a deer in the Rocky Mountains takes the cry of the Steller's jay? Whether they heard it or not, Lewis controlled his nerves against the slightest quivering. He barely breathed as he "lay looking death in the eye." Tall weeds as well as bushes and briars were all around him. He was aware of three Indians passing over the great fallen tree, several feet away from his hidden body.

After they could no longer be heard and while he continued in his frozen position, though he could not know whether the Indians had gone on or were, like animals lying in wait for prey, keeping motionless and silent, the rattlesnake uncoiled and, "passing directly over his body," disappeared in the rank growth. Lewis heard the Indians again, but they were farther off. He lay there a while relaxing and feeling thankful for deliverance from immediate danger. He had eaten little for days, and when he roused, hunger gnawed at all his vitals. After he had made his long, slow way home, unshod, unarmed, without knife, flint or fire, living mostly on roots and frogs, he said that in the first rage of hunger he thought how good rattlesnake meat is to an empty belly but would rather have died than make a meal of the snake that doubly saved his life — first by not striking, and then by keeping him motionless.

The most dramatic of all encounters between trail drivers and horseback Indians was in 1867 on the Goodnight-Loving Trail, which led from Palo Pinto County, Texas, to Fort Sumner, New Mexico. The episode has been told many times.

Charles Goodnight, thirty-one years old, and Oliver Loving, fifty-four, were partners on this drive. They had a fight with Comanches soon after setting out from their home range and lost one hundred and sixty head of cattle to them; at Horsehead Crossing on the Pecos they lost three hundred more to more Comanches. After they had trailed up the Pecos several days, free from Indians, Loving, with One-Armed Bill Wilson as escort, rode on ahead to see about contracts with army beef-buyers.

They rode a night, rested a day, and rode another night without any sign of Indians. Then Loving decided they were being unnecessarily cautious and had as well ride in daylight. That afternoon, following high ground out from the Pecos, they saw a horde of Comanches rushing towards them. After a four-mile run they got under the riverbank among sand dunes, weeds, and cane. The Indians soon had their horses. One bullet entered Loving's side and another broke an arm.

Now they were against the bank, out of sight and shot of Indians from above, and hidden by the cane and other growth from Indians who had followed them down to the lower bed of the river.

In 1926 I spent three days and nights with Colonel Goodnight, then ninety years old, on his ranch, interviewing him for a magazine article. My script quotes him as follows:

"For hours Wilson and Loving hugged the ground. One Indian more daring than the others began creeping towards them, parting the weeds and cane ahead of him with a long spear. Wilson saw the shaking cane and prepared to greet him, but knew that the moment he shot, the whole pack would rush forward. He waited.

"Then a giant rattler began to whir ahead of the spear — he sidled into view, all the while looking back toward the Indian. The Indian retreated and the rattlesnake passed unharmed almost over Wilson's leg. Neither man moved a muscle."

Goodnight, by the time I saw him, had been interviewed by other writers and had had several accounts of his trail-driving experiences published under his own name. In some of these accounts dealing with the drive up the Pecos, the rattlesnake is not even mentioned.

One-Armed Bill Wilson provided a "Narrative" for that meaty anthology of personal accounts entitled *The Trail Drivers of Texas* (Bandera, Texas, 1920). These are his words as printed: "An Indian with a long lance came crawling along, parting the weeds with his lance as he came, and just about the time I had determined to pull the trigger, he scared up a big rattlesnake. The snake came out rattling, looking back at the Indian, and coiled up right near us. The Indian, who still had not seen us, evidently got scared at the rattlesnake and turned back."

In J. Evetts Haley's biography of Goodnight (1936), based on various sources in addition to Goodnight's relations, the rattlesnake acts in accordance with the preceding accounts. Madeline Mayercord, great-granddaughter of Oliver Loving, wrote a sketch on him for the *Southwest Review*, Spring, 1936, based partly on family tradition, that leaves the rattlesnake unmentioned.

But imagination is always wanting the rider to hang over the edge of the precipice before he escapes falling to death. Imagination is always wanting the clock to strike twelve — the "knell that summons thee to heaven or to hell." One of the trail hands with Goodnight and Loving on the drive up the Pecos was H. C. Holloway. In 1895, while he was living in Fort Worth, one of the landmark books chronicling cattle history, *Historical and Biographical Record of the Cattle Industry and Cattlemen of Texas and Adjacent Territory*, was published. A sketch on Oliver

Loving in this book includes a rather long and wordy account by Holloway, which he probably did not write. Here is Holloway's version.

Firing by the Indians had ceased and all was quiet. Loving had lost much blood and was growing faint. Wilson, with legs drawn up, was lying on his armless side, grasping his six-shooter in his one hand. After a long time of stillness they heard a stirring in the cane fifteen or twenty feet away. The sounds seemed to be made by an Indian crawling towards them with a spear. Then they heard the loud rattling of what had to be a big rattlesnake.

The stirring in the cane ceased, but the rattling came nearer, and then the rattler crawled into view. Both Wilson and Loving remained absolutely still. If either stirred the cane tops, the waiting Indian might find his target. The rattlesnake came on and "coiled itself up in the lap of Wilson, its head not more than twelve inches from Wilson's face."

Shortly after this the hidden men heard the Indian receding. Again all was still, including the rattler. After a while Wilson "began moving his upper knee slightly, until he saw the snake turn its attention towards his knee." Soon it began to crawl off "around his knee, across his feet," and then into the cane.

There is a lot more to the story — Wilson's escape in the night, barefooted, dressed only in underwear, and his walk through thorns and rocks back down the river to meet Goodnight and final rescue; Loving's waiting until the Comanches had vanished and then being found by Mexicans, who took him to Fort Sumner, where he soon died of gangrene. I wonder how close that rattlesnake did get to One-Armed Bill Wilson, and I'd like to know how long it was.

In the light of a September dawn in 1868, a year after the rattlesnake got so close to One-Armed Bill Wilson on the Pecos, General George A. Forsythe and one of his sentries heard hoofbeats and then saw warbonnets on the ridge above their camp against the Arickaree Fork of the Republican River in western Kansas. Forsythe's detachment was made up of fifty scouts, along with a surgeon and Lieutenant Fred Beecher. As it soon developed, about nine hundred Cheyenne and Sioux warriors surrounded them. They took refuge on a sandbar in the river — and named it Beecher Island for the lieutenant who was killed there.

With tin plates the men dug pits for their bodies, used slain horses — not one was left alive — for breastworks, and, at the cost of five dead and eighteen wounded, stood off repeated charges. Their rations ran out, and, reduced to eating rotten horseflesh and one coyote that had trotted near, the survivors stood the Indians off for eight days, until rescue came.

On the first night Forsythe selected an old trapper named Pete Trudeau and a lad named Jack Stillwell to go to Fort Wallace, towards a hundred miles away, for reinforcements. They wore moccasins made from their boot tops so as not to leave white man tracks and had blankets wrapped around their bodies in Indian style. After crawling through the shallow water and then through tall grass on a hill, where Indian movement halted them many times, they concealed themselves at daylight at the head of a gully overgrown by high bunch grass and sunflowers. They estimated they had made about three miles. They were provided with canteens of water and horsemeat. All day they listened to gunfire at Beecher Island behind them.

The second night they crawled and skulked to the South Republican, diverted on their way by sight of two mounted parties of warriors. There seemed to be much movement of Indians. At daybreak they discovered that they were only half a mile from an Indian camp. They got into tall grass growing in a slough against the river and there spent the second day. Once some warriors stopped not thirty feet from them to water their horses. All day they heard in the camp tom-toms and cries of mourning over warriors slain at the battleground.

When night came, they crossed the South Republican, going south, and by daylight were far enough out on the prairie, they thought, to keep on traveling. About an hour after sunrise they saw coming towards them the advance guard of what proved to be a party of Cheyennes. The two scouts were down flat in the grass before the enemy had a chance to discover them. Not far away was a clump of "yellow weeds" that, as it turned out, had been fertilized by the carcasses of two buffaloes. According to some accounts, there was only one buffalo carcass. Anyhow, dried hide still covered the upper ribs of the carcass or carcasses, and the scouts crawled under it as best they could, hoping that the weeds would conceal whatever of their bodies the rawhide roof did not.

According to *Personal Recollections and Observations* of General Nelson A. Miles, "one Indian scout approached very near during the morning, scanning the country in all directions for over half an hour." According to another old army Indian-fighter, Captain R. G. Carter, some Indians came so near that "they either sat down on the carcass or leaned against it."

While the Indians were plenty near and the scouts were scrouged up under the sun-dried buffalo hide, a rattlesnake crawled under it. The sun by now was hot, a time when rattlesnakes habitually take to shade. This rattler did not coil or rattle, but he was uncomfortably near, he was in motion, and he appeared to be dissatisfied with something. Any sound or movement made by the hiders would have summoned the Indians.

Jack Stillwell was chewing tobacco and at this juncture had a mouthful of spit. He was an expert shot. He shot the "amber" straight into the rattlesnake's eyes, and the snake immediately went outside.

After a while the Indians left, and then Pete Trudeau went loco. He wanted to shout and sing, and it was only by the greatest efforts that Stillwell pacified him. After dark they got to a stream and the water brought the old trapper back to himself. They finally reached Fort Wallace. The rescue of Forsythe's men on the ninth day of their ordeal has nothing to do with a rattlesnake. In his narratives Forsythe barely mentions the snake and does not have much to say about the scouts.

In the fall of 1933 John Neal Watson of Mineral Wells, while enrolled in my course on Life and Literature of the Southwest at the University of Texas, turned in a narrative entitled "Abner Whistler's Snake Story." It was so interesting that I suggested sending it to the *Southwest Review*. It has never lost its fascination for me. It introduced me to the rattlesnake-Indian dilemma. Watson had, in his own way, elaborated characters, setting and incidents of a traditional tale of pioneer days. Somebody in Fort Worth later told me the skeleton of the tradition. In brief, here is "Abner Whistler's Snake Story."

Back in the '70's a frontiersman named Abner Whistler was ranching in the Double Mountain country, on the Double Mountain Fork of the Brazos River. Cattle rustlers were molesting him until a shot-up, broken-legged Mexican named Jesús María showed up at his ranch one night and found a kind refuge. Whistler afterwards figured that Jesús María had been one of the cattle thieves; anyhow, they quit driving off his stock. The Mexican was a good cowhand, and no man could have been more loyal to another than he was to the rancher who had taken him in, but his broken leg never did get strong enough for him to more than hobble on it.

About sundown one July day, after Whistler and Jesús had been chasing cattle in rough country and their horses were weary, they were driving a small bunch of cows and calves back to their home range when a band of Comanches swooped down on them, yelling and shooting. There was nothing for them to do but try to outrun the Comanches. They might have done it, for the Indians' horses were half-starved and weak, but an arrow went into the Mexican's horse at the flank and soon he crumpled down.

Jesús did not want his patrón to stop and take him on, but Whistler pulled him up behind himself without pausing to argue. He was making for a cave up the slope of Double Mountain. He had not been in it and had seen it only once, by accident, for the mouth was almost completely screened by scrub cedars. His landmark was a bench of flat reddish ground contouring the hill. In front and a little to one side of the cave grew an unusually large cedar. The rough land and the double load slowed his horse down so much that after riding a short distance he decided to make for the cave afoot. The Comanches were still far enough behind that they could hardly keep sight of a man on foot in that tumbled, cedar-studded ground. Whistler judged that he wouldn't have to go far before sighting the place.

As he jumped to the ground, Jesús with him, he jerked

the bridle off his horse, headed him downhill and gave him a rap across the rump with the reins. Then, partly carrying Jesús, he followed the compass inside his body. Just as he came in sight of the big cedar, he heard fresh yells below and knew the Comanches had come upon his horse. In a little while he and Jesús were in the cave. Continued yelling told him that the Comanches were searching the gullies downhill. The stony soil and dimming daylight had kept them from following the trail of the two men, but they soon turned uphill, trying to hound it out.

At dusk the Comanches made camp at the big cedar in front of the cave. There was not much likelihood that they would hunt further before morning. A full moon was rising. The cave was about five feet high at its mouth, too low for comfortable standing, and sloped back sharply. The smooth rock floor made a good sitting or lying-down place. As Abner Whistler later realized, it appeared to have been polished by some form of life.

The Indians made a low fire, half-cooked some meat, ate it with satisfied grunts, and then, except for three warriors who kept watch on their horses, lay down to sleep. While all this was going on, Whistler whispered to Jesús that he should remain in hiding while he, of strong legs, slipped out and made for the Swenson ranch, about fifteen miles to the west.

He was about to take his chance on crawling out through the cedars, and the two were standing, bent over, at the mouth of the cave, when they heard a barely audible sound from behind them — the sound of slow slithering on smooth rock. Then, in the filtered moonlight, they saw, at their feet, about the biggest diamondback anybody ever saw in the breaks of the Brazos — which has always been a noted rattlesnake country.

The big snake was not rattling. It seemed unaware of the motionless men. It stopped, stretched out in the moonlight. Maybe it would crawl out soon and hunt for a cottontail rabbit, a rat, or something else to eat — but snakes eat only at long intervals. This one just stayed where it was. Whistler had his hand on his six-shooter but realized that a shot would bring the reckless Comanches. As he shifted weight on his feet without moving them and felt his head against the low, jagged roof of the cave, he missed the hat he had lost to a limb before he abandoned his horse. The longer he stood bumping his head, the more he missed it.

Meanwhile, the big diamondback hardly moved. It was the hour for snakes to come out. Seemingly crawling from crevices far back in the cave, they now congregated on the smooth rock at its mouth. The slickness of the pavement indicated that the cave had been a rattlesnake den for perhaps centuries. Silently, smoothly, the rattlers crawled around and over the feet of the stooped men. Whistler wore boots, but Jesús wore only moccasins. He could not pull a boot over his crippled foot.

The cramped men's only relief was to press harder against the roof. Abner Whistler, as he later related, became so cramped that the one desirable thing in life seemed to him to lie down, even with rattlesnakes. But he stood on. He was taller than the Mexican and, therefore, more bent over, but the Mexican had only one sound leg. Finally Whistler asked him if he had rather die there by the snakes or make a dash and have the Indians upon him.

The Mexican always addressed Whistler as Salvador — Saver, Saviour. "Salvador," he said, "I am old and you are young. In a little while I am going to fall and rest. When I do and the snakes bite me, you jump." Then he put a trembling hand to Whistler's face, whispered adiós, and fell. Instantly the snakes were rattling and striking him. He had fallen as far away from his Salvador as he could.

Whistler did not jump. There seemed to be snakes everywhere. He knew that with the coolness of predawn they would go inside to warmth. About four o'clock they vanished, the big diamondback last of all.

The moon was still shining at dawn. Whistler's back and legs were so stiff that he had to use both hands to help a leg move. A clear view told him that the Comanches were all gone. They had left while he was absorbed with pain and terror. Old Jesús lay there as cold as marble.

Not much is down in writing about Jeff Turner the Indian Hater, but in frontier households his was once a familiar name. Many white people considered him a monomaniac, which he was; Indians looked upon him as a devil,

which he was also. The only description of him that I have
found is in John C. Duval's *The Adventures of Bigfoot
Wallace*, wherein old Bigfoot does most of the talking.

Jeff Turner, he said, "was as curious a looking specimen as I ever saw in any country. He was tall, spare-built,
dressed in buckskin shirt and leggins, and wore a coonskin
cap. His hair was matted together and hung around his
neck and over his eyes in great swabs, and his eyes peered
out from them as bright as a couple of mesquite coals. I
have seen all sorts of eyes — panther, wolf, catamount,
leopard — but I never saw eyes that glittered and flashed
and danced about like those in that man's head. He rode a
raw-boned, vicious-looking horse named Pepper-Pod, and
carried a long, old-fashioned flint-and-steel Kentucky rifle
on his shoulder or across his saddle."

Turner had come to Texas from Kentucky and settled
on the Guadalupe River with his wife and three small
boys. One day he came in from a hunt to find all four dead
and Indians scalping them. He got four Indians and after
that lived for the one purpose of killing and scalping
more Indians. He could be counted on to join any expedi-
tion against them, but habitually hunted and waylaid them
alone. His type was rare, but he had precedents. "Mad
Anne" Bailey of Virginia (1747-1825) was perhaps the
most noted; after her husband was killed by Indians she
lived only to avenge. Charles Goodnight used to tell of
coming one rainy night upon a solitary frontiersman in his
cabin curing a freshly taken Indian scalp over the fire; in

retribution for a daughter killed by Indians while she was suckling a baby, he cherished a collection of these well-preserved trophies. Any dedicated hater is a warped abnormality. The haters represented by Jeff Turner are not to be classed among those murderous scalpers for bounty led by Santiago (James) Kirker and John Glanton, who in Chihuahua and Sonora collected not only on Apache scalps but on equally dark hair from innocent Mexican citizens.

Jeff Turner's career of single-minded vengeance began some time before Texas became a state. He told Bigfoot Wallace that whenever he had to go a long spell without lifting hair he got to feeling "peculiar." During the preceding ten years, he said, he had hung up forty-six scalps in his camp, but wouldn't "die satisfied until he had a cool hundred."

How many scalps Jeff Turner got before he died, I have no idea. How he died is in the realm of tradition. One December night in 1932 while I was in a hotel in El Paso, a vigorous knocking made me jump to my feet. When I opened the door, the frame was filled with man, over six feet of him, all in powerful proportions, wearing an enormous Western hat not at all disproportionate to the wearer. The man was Frank Collinson, now dead. In the early '70's he had come from England to Texas, where he took with gusto to mustanging, buffalo-hunting, ranching and other forms of open range life. He had a background of reading and the perspective of civilization, and in his latter years he wrote considerably for Western magazines.

That night before he sat down in a big chair in my hotel room, he began talking. After a while he asked if I had known Bigfoot Wallace. I hadn't. He had — on the Medina River, west of San Antonio, where Bigfoot batched alone.

"Did you ever hear of Jeff Turner the Indian Hater?" Frank Collinson asked.

"Yes," I replied, "I have read about him in Duval's book on Bigfoot Wallace."

"Does the book tell what became of Jeff Turner?"

"No, and I have often wondered."

"Well, Bigfoot told me. He said that Turner kept on hounding Indians, picking off one when he could and saving the scalp, until one night they found him out in the brush asleep. He was too valuable to kill right there. They took him to their camp, where the wife of a chief was soon to give birth to a baby — a boy they hoped. They spread-eagled Jeff Turner on the ground and sat this chief's wife down beside him. Then the chief cut out Turner's heart and while it was still palpitating gave it to her to eat hot and raw. The belief was that Turner's bravery would thus be transferred to the unborn child."

When I heard this story, I understood why Duval, who belonged to the Victorian age and who wrote his books originally for publication in a magazine for boys and girls, did not tell what became of Jeff Turner. But maybe that's just a story; again, maybe it's fact.

In a book entitled *The Quirt and the Spur* (Chicago,

1909) by Edgar Rye, the ending of Jeff Turner the Indian Hater is bound to rattlesnakes. Rye was a frontier newspaper editor; he could do nearly everything but stick to facts. Not that he was averse to facts, but if they were not handy or suitable to the dramatic, he frequently used something else. His book, which centers around Fort Griffin during buffalo days, contains real characters and realistic facts along with fabrications and a lot of talk in quotation marks that is absurdly false to life. An oddity in the book named Smoky tells what follows, here much abbreviated.

About the time the Civil War closed, Smoky, ranging alone in the Fort Phantom Hill country, fell in with Jeff Turner. As usual, he was hunting scalps, and plenty of scalps were around. While they were trying to save a fool camped out in the open with his wagon and family on the Clear Fork of the Brazos, a band of Comanches turned the tables on them. The two frontiersmen killed two and got away in darkness.

With the Indians hot behind, Smoky and Turner took off up what proved to be a boxed canyon. They couldn't turn back down the canyon; they couldn't climb out of it; and now, the sure-of-victory Indians yelling on their trail like bloodhounds, they came to the head of it. Feeling in the darkness, Smoky discovered a hole, about as big around as a barrel, in the blockading wall overhead. They pulled up into it and found themselves in what Jeff Turner called a "kind of underground prairie." The ceiling to it was so low that they had to crawl to move about; the floor was "damp and slimy."

After they had crawled back a way, they heard in the dense darkness the bloodcurdling rattle of a rattlesnake. Anybody who, in darkness, has ever heard that rattling almost at his feet will agree that it curdles the blood. They halted motionless. Smoky knew that Jeff Turner had a box of Mexican wax matches, which burn like miniature tapers. He whispered to Turner to strike one. Turner lit it.

They saw "not more than ten feet away a wriggling mass of writhing, twisting rattlesnakes" untangling themselves and crawling off in all directions. The men, resting at the moment on their knees, remained as if paralyzed, not moving even to strike another match. Darkness could be no deeper; tensity could be no tenser. Finally, after what seemed an immeasurable time of immobile kneeling, Turner's cramped muscles must have made him relax. He moved to shift his weight.

There was a whir, and then he said, "Smoky, I have lifted my last scalp."

In a little while he began to twist about and to rave. Presently he grabbed Smoky by the arm and said in a hoarse, thick voice, "Look! there's a hole in the ground right in front of me. It's the skylight to hell, and I wonder why the devil left it uncovered." Then in extravagancies that would have satisfied any exhorter holding sinners over brimstone furnaces, he described his own advance into the torture of heat and the power of hellish beings.

He died about the time a dim light told Smoky which way to get back to the mouth of the cave. Before this, he knew not when, the rattlesnakes had vanished. The Comanches also had left the canyon. Smoky buried what was left of Jeff Turner the Indian Hater within sight of the ghostly chimneys that still mark the site of Fort Phantom Hill.

Snake-Killing Cats and Dogs

FOR YEARS I HAVE KEPT a letter written by Mrs. J. R. Thompson of Lancaster, Texas. One night in Alabama when she was a little girl, sixty-five years before she wrote me, the family cat, Katie by name, brought in a live blacksnake for her kittens. The snake was numb but could wriggle. Katie seems to have been a good provider.

"I do not recall," Mrs. Thompson's letter reads, "her ever bringing in a poisonous snake, but mice, scorpions, scaly lizards, sun-runners, more blacksnakes, garter snakes and even butterflies and large grasshoppers she put on her table — a shelf outside our window — for the kittens.

"Katie disappeared for six months or longer once when she was about two years old. We children were desolated, and then one morning Katie was back. Sometime after this she became ill. She had no appetite or she could not swallow. We tried tempting her with everything we could think of. She only grew weaker. Then as a last resort one of us caught a cricket and put it before her. She ate it.

"For days afterwards we roamed the grounds around

our house hunting crickets. She would follow us and, whenever we clapped down a hat or a bonnet over a cricket, she was right there to catch it. She recovered, and we children vowed we'd never again kill a cricket unless it was for Katie. We've kept our vow.

"We had an English coach dog named Kino who seemed to take particular pleasure in killing rattlesnakes. I saw him kill a large one once. He would circle it, making short grabs and barking furiously. After dodging strike after strike, he finally grabbed the snake by the back of the neck and, biting down hard, shook it to death."

I've never seen a cat or a dog kill any kind of snake, but I've heard other testimony to the effect that the dog catches the snake just back of the head. This is not precisely the technique described by Mr. William Allen Maddox in an interesting book entitled *Historical Carvings in Leather*, published by the Naylor Company of San Antonio. According to Mr. Maddox, their family dog named Shep would circle around and around the rattlesnake, barking excitedly while the snake rattled, getting closer and closer in his circles and inducing the snake to strike at him but always dodging the strike. After the snake had struck as far as he could, Shep would spring forward and "grab him about the middle of the body; then he would shake him for all he was worth. When he laid the snake down, there were usually one piece in his mouth and two other pieces out on the ground in opposite directions."

According to Mr. Maddox, a dog usually has to be bitten at least once to become cautious enough to be expert at snake-killing. One young dog he owned had learned to kill snakes with old dogs and had not been bitten until he got his lesson. He would dodge a rattler's strike just as any dog will dodge a blow. "One day while I was taking a drink of water to my father plowing in a field, this dog and I encountered a large rattlesnake. The young dog made short work of him. The head came off with three or four inches of snake, and rolled within about six feet of me. The dog seemed to be proud of his achievement and went around smelling of the pieces. I was examining the snake's rattles and never noticed the dog until it was too late. The mouth of the snake was wide open and when this foolish young dog stuck his nose into the jaws, they contracted. He ran backwards pawing at his nose with both forefeet. He finally raked his head free of the fangs. Before we could get to the house it was swollen badly. My mother gave him all the fat meat he could eat. He was sick for several days, his head swelled out of proportion. After he got well, he had it in for all snakes, and never seemed so happy as when killing them. He was not bitten a second time."

In 1938 an old-time cowman named W. H. Hamilton had an autobiography published in *South Dakota Historical Collections*. Herein he tells of a greyhound, one of a pack, that seemed unable to learn how to fight rattlesnakes. "The first time he was bitten," recorded W. H. Hamilton, "I was sure he would die. His head swelled so badly he could not chew or swallow for several days, and he spent all this time lying in the mud down at the creek. He was the only dog we had which would grab a snake while it was coiled. We had others that would kill snakes, but they would always wait until the snake started to crawl, and then grab it and shake it to pieces. I think this dog became immune to snake venom, for he got so it affected him very little when bitten."

Not long ago my friend Arthur Woodward of California, while on a visit to me here in Austin, dictated the following account of a cat's technique in fighting rattlesnakes.

"In the summer of 1908 when I was about ten years old, my family moved from Iowa to California and were living in the little town of Ramona, about thirty-eight miles northeast of San Diego. Our house was frame, painted green, up on a rock foundation high enough for one to crawl under it. I had never seen a rattlesnake — never heard one. Sitting by the window one day, roses outside and bees in the roses, I kept hearing an insistent buzz above the bee-loudness. I'd hear a cat's *meow* and then a buzz. I told my dad, 'I think a rattlesnake's out there.'

" 'No, that's bees — no rattlesnake,' he said.

"I said, 'I hear something that's not bees.' I went out and looked under the house. Our old cat had her three kittens lined up in a row, though they were lying down, while she fought a little rattler about a foot long. It was rattling, and the kittens were fidgety. Every time one of them made a move forward, the old cat would reach back and knock it galley-west, clear away from that snake. She would wait until the snake struck, and then she would hit right behind the head and knock it. She kept knocking it out farther in the open and finally knocked it clear out from under the house. We killed it, but she could have killed it by herself, no doubt. Every time it struck at her, she would hit it just behind the head."

A Bola of Rattlesnakes

S O MANY THINGS HAPPEN in the fall that I wonder why Julius Caesar didn't fix the beginning of the calendar year at this time instead of in the standstill time of mid-winter. Fall is the time for all sorts of changes. It is the time when rattlesnakes change their dispositions and are drawn towards their dens as instinctively as birds migrate.

In a caveless country like the coastal plains of Texas, rattlesnakes do not gather in large numbers to hibernate in a common den; they scatter into badger holes, rat nests, and other coverts. Yet they seem to have a tendency, per-haps only sporadically exercised, to congregate before moving. Birds, which are biologically descended from snakes, may have inherited the tendency. Certainly they exercise it with more regularity. The great, restless con-gregations of birds of many species before migrating are one of the spectacles of nature. The congregations of rat-tlesnakes are equally spectacular, though only a few people have reported the sight.

I spent Christmas in the year 1932 at Cusihuiriachic, Chihuahua, west of Chihuahua City, as guest of the manager of the Cusihuiriachic Mining Company. There I met the most vivid reporter of rattlesnake gatherings I have ever come across. He was the Cusi Company's doctor, F. R. Seyffert. In blood he was one-quarter German and three-quarters Spanish, having been born in Mexico. He had been educated in medicine in the United States, was scientific-minded, and at the time I knew him was about sixty-five years old. He had spent most of his life in the mountains of Mexico, and was as familiar with pack mules, prospector's hopes, native folklore, and canyon trails as he was with femurs and gastric juices. He was quiet and precise in speech, rather sympathetic towards wonders in this world — as I am also. When I recall his talk now, my heart leaps up with joy, it was so interesting to me. Immediately after he gave me the accounts of rattlesnake gatherings that follow this introduction, I wrote them down — on Christmas Eve night.

"On September 15, 1898," Dr. Seyffert said, "I was riding between Santa Rosalia and Arenosas, on the edge of the Bolsón de Mapimí of Chihuahua. After leaving Santa Rosalia on the Conchos River I entered a sandy country abounding in prairie dogs and rattlesnakes. I saw a rattlesnake and got down off my horse to cut a mesquite switch to kill it. I had been on a medical call and had no pistol or rifle. It is troublesome, as you know, to cut any good-sized switch of the thorny mesquite with a pocketknife. After I had cut it, I looked where I had seen the snake and it was no longer there, though its trail in the sand was plain. I am not expert enough to tell from a snake's trail which direction it has taken. I made no effort to hunt the snake down.

"I turned towards my horse and had taken but a few steps when I saw another rattler. I killed it. As I looked up, I saw another; I killed it. Then another, and I killed it. As I recalled later, all three of these snakes were, when I first saw them, crawling towards a shallow gully, maybe two feet deep and several feet wide. The third rattler I killed was almost on the edge of the gully.

"When my attention was free and I looked over into the gully, I saw a sight that literally froze my blood and made my hair stand on end. There, almost at my feet, was a writhing, squirming mass of rattlesnakes, hundreds of them it seemed to me. The twisted, twisting bola (ball) they made was certainly two and a half feet in diameter. It was a solid mass of rattlesnake bodies, and rattlesnakes all around it were somehow entangling themselves with the bola. The snakes were not rattling; they were just crawling and writhing.

"I ran to my horse, mounted and left. It is a common belief among the Mexicans that rattlesnakes gather in this way during their rutting season, in the fall."

According to scientists, rattlesnakes mate in the spring. I have never seen them mate, though I have talked to men who have. Can anybody who has seen rattlesnakes mate be sure of the time of year?

"I am sure of the date on which I saw this bola of rattlesnakes," Dr. Seyffert went on. "I have never kept diaries, but I know that I made the ride the day before the Diez y Seis — September the Sixteenth — celebration.

"An experience narrated to me by Francisco Delgado, a rancher near Cusihuiriachic, corroborates the phenomenon I have described. Delgado, accompanied by a servant, was on the trail to Batopilas, Chihuahua, with some pack mules. One noon after they had lunched and let the mules graze awhile, Delgado told his mozo to go bring in the animals. They were not far off. Delgado put the coffeepot and other lunch things in a morral and went to adjusting something about one of the pack saddles. He paid no attention to where the mozo had gone.

"Presently he heard a cry of distress. He recognized the voice as coming from the servant. Nobody else could be crying out in that immense solitude anyhow. He looked but could see no human being. His hand was on his pistol when he heard a second cry of distress, fainter than the first. It gave him the direction, however, and he ran towards it. It seemed to come from a dry arroyo, and he saw two of the mules on the other side of the arroyo.

"When he came to where he could look down into the arroyo, he saw the man stretched out flat. He was already dead. He was amid hundreds of rattlesnakes. Some were crawling over him. Most of them were in a great bola towards which the others were squirming. The man, meaning to go across the arroyo to bring back the mules, must have jumped into it without noticing the snakes that he landed among. What brought them together only one

[149]

who can interpret the overpowering impulses of nature can say."

In an autobiography entitled *Pony Trails in Wyoming* (published in 1941), John K. Rollinson tells of a ball of rattlesnakes he saw on the Platte River one fall day, seemingly in 1898.

"At noon," he says, "we camped within about two miles of the Rock ranch on the Platte. While camp was being made for dinner, I rode out to some low sandstone rocks to get a better view. My horse shied at an object that appeared at first glance to be a dark-colored rock. A second look disclosed a bunch of rattlesnakes, all intertwisted into a huge ball, almost the size of a watermelon. . . . They were denning up for the winter, and those that were struggling to get free were headed for a hole in the rocks. I signaled to one of the riders to come there. Neither of us had a gun at the time; so we cautiously climbed off our suspicious horses and threw rocks at the mass of rattlers. Those that were not too cold wriggled down into the hole. We killed three. Then we rode back to camp and told the others what we had seen. Some doubted our story. Some said that on late fall days they had seen similar balls of snakes ready to den up in the rocks."

Well, how big is a watermelon?

One of the excellent natural history publications of America is the journal of the Zoological Society of Philadelphia. In an issue some time back devoted mostly to the rattlesnake, an authority, after remarking on the good that rattlesnakes do by destroying rodents, concludes:

"It might be argued, aside from practical reasons, that there are people who like rattlesnakes and enjoy seeing these splendid animals, these examples of evolutionary perfection, in their natural state. This minority is increasing as the ignorance and misconceptions concerning snakes are being dispelled."

I am good at belonging to minorities and I have joined this one. I have killed hundreds of rattlesnakes. The next one I meet I think I shall tell how much I appreciate him. There are legions of morons driving around in automobiles over the country more dangerous and less interesting. Why should I pick on rattlesnakes?

Do Rattlesnakes Swallow Their Young?

THERE ARE AT LEAST two reasons why I would not want to live in Ireland. One of them is that there are no snakes in Ireland. I wouldn't kill a harmless snake any more than I would kill a wren. Rattlesnakes, though not harmless, are the most interesting of all snakes in North America. I hate to think of the day when there won't be any. They make the country more interesting and more natural. After all these generations of civilized man's association with them, there are several things about them that not even the most scientific naturalists know.

Do they swallow their young? By asking that question and not flatly denying it, I — in the eyes of literalistic scientists — lay bare my credulity and ignorance. I don't care. Anyhow, popular testimony concerning this phenomenon interests me. Until very recently the scientists denied that roadrunners kill rattlesnakes. Now they have to admit the fact. I assert nothing. I merely transmit.

Nobody who has ever known Bill Gates, slow-talking,

tall, angular, old-time cowboy, all the juices of fancy long ago dried out of him by the winds and suns of the plains, would suspect that his clear eyes had ever seen air-drawn daggers. I met him in Midland in 1934. He told me that while he was poisoning prairie dogs in Andrews County in 1920, he was nearing a dog hole to put some poisoned grain around it when he saw a good-sized rattlesnake right at the mouth of it. Then he saw several small rattlesnakes near the old one. The big rattlesnake saw him, went to rattling and opened its mouth, whereupon the little ones ran into it. Gates killed the old snake, he said, cut it open and killed the little ones hiding inside.

Dr. F. R. Seyffert, of the Cusihuiriachic Mining Company, gave me several instances of folk belief, as such, among Indians of the Sierra Madre and impressed me as being aware of the distinction between fact and fancy. After each of two or three talks I had with Dr. Seyffert, I immediately set down what I wanted to remember. The account that follows is almost exactly in his own words.

"In the year 1883, the year before I left Mexico to study in Washington University, at Saint Louis, I was walking one morning through our vegetable garden, at Yoquivo, Chihuahua. I was traversing some rows of dried potato vines when I saw a very small snake that appeared to have a rattle on the end of its tail — just one rattle, a button. It had gone but a short distance, and I was following it eagerly, when I heard a kind of whistle. I repeat, a kind of whistle. I was facing the source of this singular sound, which I knew came from nobody about the garden and which seemed to come up from the ground.

"It did come up from the ground. It came from a large rattlesnake — a female as I was soon to learn — lying between two potato rows, just ahead of me, with mouth wide open. Her color blended so perfectly with the ground and she was so still that I might have stepped on her without seeing her if it had not been for the whistling sound. Keeping my eye on her so as not to lose her, I reached for a clod, the ground being of a clayey nature. I had found a good clod and was raising up to advance one step nearer and strike, when I saw the little snake I had roused and had been keeping in sight dash into the old one's mouth. Instantly it was followed by a second little snake, then a third. I threw the clod, mashing the head of the mother rattler. I was exceedingly curious to examine her insides.

"I speared the head with my pocketknife, which had a long blade, and on it carried the snake to an old adobe wall that had been weathered down to about the height suitable for an operating table. I laid the snake on this wall and drove a sharp stick through the head into the adobe. Then withdrawing my knife with one hand and holding the snake's tail taut with the other, I split its belly open. Five little snakes came out, each with a button.

"This is the only time I have ever seen this snake-swallowing phenomenon. I have not known anyone else who has seen it. I read of it in a book by a German naturalist. I tell only what I have experienced with my own eyes."

Now I quote from a letter by Hardin H. Jones, of Brady, Texas: "My experience was at the Texas National Guard camp at Palacios, in August, 1927. Some of the boys, while cleaning up the officers' mess hall, had killed a rattlesnake and were bringing it down our company street, on the way to the trash pile. I and several other boys saw the snake and, of course, wanted to examine it. The fellow who was carrying it threw it on the ground. In order to examine the fangs, I picked up two small sticks and prized open the snake's mouth. Then I noticed a peculiar color down the snake's throat. I raked with one of the sticks and brought out a tiny rattlesnake. In like manner I raked out three more. That is all I saw. The little ones were in the lower part of the snake's mouth, just above the throat. They had not been swallowed. They were from three to three and a half inches long, had the diamond markings rather indistinct, with a slight yellow tinge, and each had a button at the end of its tail. I do not know whether the old snake was male or female; it was about three feet long and had, as I recall, eight rattles. By going over the roster of the Service Company, from Brownwood, of the 142nd Infantry of the Texas National Guard camped at Palacios in 1927, several witnesses to corroborate this testimony might be found.

"Mr. John Fullager, of Lohn, Texas, tells me that he once cut open two large rattlesnakes he had killed together and found young unborn snakes in each."

Hardin Jones, author of the foregoing account, has an inquiring mind and is especially interested in Texas history. He makes it clear that he did not see any little snakes swallowed. On April 27, 1935, he wrote me another letter relaying the testimony of a fence-builder, trapper and all-around outdoors laborer named John E. Morris.

"In the spring of 1905 or 1906, Morris was building a fence on the C. P. Gray ranch on the San Saba River in McCulloch County. One day as he was nearing a small thicket, he heard a short rattle, then another short rattle — just one or two r-r-rs. When he located the snake she had her mouth open, and a little snake was just going in. She closed her mouth and opened it again, and another little one ran in. She opened and closed her mouth for each entrant until several had gone in. Morris moved closer, and the snake glided into a hole, as did several small snakes that had not got into the old one's mouth.

"Morris had spade and posthole digger in hand. He dug the old snake out and killed her, also five or six small snakes. He cut the old one open and exposed fifteen or twenty small snakes, all in a ball, tangled up and wriggling like a can of worms. They were about six inches long, each with a button, and they attempted to fight."

Only in one other source have I met the description of the little snakes as being massed. This is in a brief sketch by Ernest E. Hubert in the *Frontier and Midland Magazine*, published at Missoula, Montana, March, 1934. Hubert was surveying in the Badlands.

"It had become a habit with us," he says, "to open up all the gorged snakes we killed. It was surprising how many field mice, kangaroo rats, chipmunks and other small rodents these reptiles could hold. Now, an unusually fat rattler hastened to wiggle out of the way. Before it could reach a hole at the base of a cactus clump, I cut off its head with my light spade.

"I held down the tail end of the still twitching body with my foot and started cutting into the cold greasy entrails when Kirby gave a sharp warning. Drawing my hands away quickly, I saw with astonishment a wiggling mass of tiny snakes pop out of the opening I had made. Darting rapidly about the body of the dead mother were six very young rattlers, perfectly formed and about eight inches long. Thrusting patches of red flannel at them, Kirby soon had those baby snakes coiling and striking. Then he began grinding his hobbed heel into the tiny, poison-filled heads.

"We had heard that the young rattlesnakes were hatched from eggs laid in the warm sands; yet here were six of them found alive within the mother's body, active and ready to defend themselves as soon as they struck the ground. We learned later that the young are hatched from eggs, but within the parent, thus giving the impression that young rattlers are swallowed by the parent."

The rattlesnake, like various other reptiles, is ovoviviparous — hatching its eggs within its own body. B. O. Grant, a schoolteacher at Ibex, Texas, knew this and had for twelve years been observing snakes from the point of view of an amateur herpetologist when in May, 1937, he saw something contrary to all herpetological teaching.

While he was walking across his pasture, he heard "a slight hissing sound" near a crevice in the hillside. Looking down into the crevice, he saw a large rattlesnake lying between two rocks and small snakes crawling into its mouth. He killed the snake with stones, and then "to prove to himself what he had often denied," he cut the snake open and removed the small ones. There were eighteen of them, from five to six inches long.

As I told Mr. Grant, it is a thousand pities that he did not tie up the parent snake's mouth and take her to town and open her up before witnesses of some anatomical knowledge. Now I quote from an article on "The Poisonous Snakes of Texas," by J. D. Mitchell, that appeared in the *Transactions of the Texas Academy of Science*, 1903.

"About May 1, 1866, at Point Comfort, Calhoun County, I was moving some palings, which had been piled on two-by-four scantlings; grass had grown around the pile, forming an ideal place for snakes. A young Negro man was assisting me; when near the bottom of the pile, we were notified by the rattling that snakes were under the pile. We slipped a scantling under one edge of the pile, and turned it over at one stroke. In one corner a large female was coiled, with small ones eight or ten inches long crawling over her and coiled around her. In another corner was coiled another large female with young ones, about half the size of the first batch, crawling over her. The young

Negro exclaimed, 'For God's sake, look! She is eating
them!' A look showed the tail of one of the smaller brood
disappear down its mother's throat. We began on them
with sticks, and soon killed the whole lot. A dissection then
followed. Snake number one was poor, but in normal condition, and had twelve young ones around her. Snake number two was poor also, and had three of her young ones in
her stomach; one was dead, having been killed by a blow
on the mother; the other two were alive; there were seven
young ones besides the three taken from the mother's
stomach; the dried egg cases were present, showing that
they had not been hatched very long. The mother snake
also had a bunch of wire worms in the abdominal cavity,
near the anus. . . .

"I know that I am flying in the face of all that I have
read about the breeding habits of Crotalus, when I say that
they deposit their eggs. I will not say that they do not
sometimes retain their eggs until hatching time and then
bring forth the young alive (for I have opened females
bearing eggs in which incubation was well under way);
but I have never witnessed this performance, whereas I
have frequently found the eggs, guarded by the mother
snake, which fought till death for their protection. It is
true that I have never found perfectly fresh eggs in a nest;
they were always ready or nearly ready to hatch, the thin
shell or envelope having lost its roundness and crinkled in
around the young snake. Another theory which may throw
some light on this point is that the writers who speak of

rattlesnakes bringing forth live young made their observations upon snakes in captivity; which condition may have had some influence upon them, causing them to retain their eggs until hatched and the young snakes to be brought forth alive. My observations were made with wild snakes in a state of nature. I will leave the reconciliation of these contradictory facts to future observers. . . .

"The female deposits her eggs in some damp, cool place. I have found them in 'cave-in' holes in the bay bank made by water; in holes in the ground at the root of bushes dug by box tortoise or some rodent; and under timber piled near the ground. I have always found the mother snake near the eggs; frequently she was coiled around the eggs and fought savagely to protect them."

When wildlife on the land was prodigal in quantity and pristine in nature, there were exceedingly few observers with the perspective of natural history. Davy Crockett was "wrathy to kill a bear," and the only genuine interest he had in bears was to satisfy the wrath to kill. Buffalo Bill won his name, not because he had any intimate knowledge of the buffalo's instincts, habits and biological nature, but merely because he was proficient in destroying the animal. Broncho Charlie claimed to have extraordinary powers over wild horses, but Gladys Shaw Erskine in writing his life could draw from him no definite information about that exceedingly interesting animal, the Spanish horse of Western ranges. The pioneer tradition towards the creatures of the earth was to kill them rather than to study them.

It developed expert trailers and deadly marksmen, but neither intellectual curiosity nor civilized sympathy towards animal life.

Joseph Daniel Mitchell, whose extraordinary statements concerning rattlesnakes have just been quoted, lived the last thirty-five years of his life at Victoria, Texas, where he died in 1922. He was born on a ranch in Calhoun County in 1848, and retired from it in middle life to read the books in his library, plant pecan trees on the public squares of Victoria, promote the city's public school system, serve in the Texas legislature, where he authored the bill establishing the present Game, Fish and Oyster Commission, and, above all, to pursue science. According to a biographical sketch published in the 88th Anniversary Number of the Victoria *Advocate* (1934), J. D. Mitchell was for seventeen years an entomologist with the United States Department of Agriculture. In 1894 he published at Victoria a twenty-two-page *List of Texas Mollusca;* for many years he corresponded with the Smithsonian Institution, sending it both data and specimens. He was certainly aware of scientific processes and aims. His own mind seems not to have been scientifically fibered, but if he created evidence, the creation must have been due to the "constructive memory" that is an unconscious possession of perhaps a majority of human beings.

A contemporary pioneer in natural history observations was Dr. Rudolph Menger, born in San Antonio in 1851. His *Texas Nature Observations and Reminiscences* was published in San Antonio in 1913. It seems not to have occurred to him to question his own statement that "the Crotalus family, as well as the moccasin snake, swallow their offspring." He had not observed the phenomenon himself, but he secured testimony on the subject from a rancher and city alderman named John Wickland, who wrote him as follows:

"In 1862, shortly after starting in the sheep business, I was herding the flock myself, and one day met a [rattle] snake apparently asleep, with a number of young ones around her, when all of a sudden they noticed me and disappeared through the old snake's mouth, and after killing her I found them inside." At another time, Wickland and a German neighbor named Adolph Real killed three thick rattlesnakes that crawled out of a burning brush pile. He cut each of them open and found "eighteen young ones in the first, eight in the second and twenty-two in the third, making forty-eight young snakes."

On September 30, 1926, my old friend John Young of Alpine, Texas, whose reminiscences I was soon to weave into *A Vaquero of the Brush Country* and who died in 1932, wrote me as follows: "I remember one time in company with John Beasley we were riding through a canebrake on Pease River trying to get a shot at a buffalo. We stopped at the edge of a small opening to look when we noticed the largest rattlesnake that I ever saw stretched out in the sun. I am sure she was at least six feet long. My partner called my attention to the little snakes around her.

They were about the size of broom straws. The old snake gave a short low whistle, threw her mouth open, when all the little snakes ran into her mouth — there must have been at least twenty-five of them. That was the best chance I ever had to kill a whole bunch of snakes. We sat there [on our horses] and held a consultation. As I remember, we only had six cartridges each and they meant life to us in more ways than one. We must kill meat to eat, and we knew there were some straggling bunches of Indians in the country. We could not afford one cartridge, although it meant to kill at least twenty-five at one shot. We then began to look around for a rock or a chunk, but there was none in sight, so we rode on."

John Young had seen the elephant and expected to look upon winged angels. He didn't believe in ghosts, but he believed strong in the Lost Nigger Mine of the Big Bend. Another frontier realist, of earlier date, was Buck Barry. He believed that possums are "borned" through the nose. Rattlesnakes, of course, interested him. In the manuscript of his *Reminiscences* is the following account:

"After they are borned, when the old snake gives alarm of danger, she will throw wide open her mouth and the little snakes run down her throat for protection. My father was riding through the woods stock hunting. He rode by the end of a hollow log where a good many little rattlers were laying in the sun. On his dismounting to investigate, the nest of little snakes fled into the log. His curiosity was so aroused he came to the house, got an axe and split open the log, finding one large snake, inside of which were sixteen — the whole nest of little snakes he saw sunning."

As mentioned earlier, I published a large part (February 8, 1942) of the foregoing testimony on rattlesnake-swallowing in four Texas newspapers. Several readers wrote me giving additional testimony, from which I published a second article in the same papers, on March 1, 1942. Further testimonials led me to publish a third article, on August 30, 1942. One of the letter-writers, Asa Jones, rancher of Brewster County, Texas, I have known the better part of my life and have a strong trust in his eyes, memory and word.

Asa Jones says: "When I was a boy twelve or thirteen years old, in Bee County, Texas, Sid Smith and I were cleaning the underbrush and a rat's nest out from around a mesquite tree we wanted to cut down for a post. We saw a sizable rattlesnake sort of sidewinding and backing down into the opening into the rat's nest, close to the trunk of the mesquite. As she backed down, this rattlesnake had her mouth open and was making a sort of blowing noise. We saw several little snakes, something like six inches long, wriggling towards her. We thought they were following her into the hole. After we had cleared the trash away and killed the old snake, we couldn't find the little ones. The rats had covered over a kind of bowl for their house, and it was in this that the snake had taken refuge, but we could not locate a hole or any other place where the little snakes could have gone.

"Then we remembered that we had heard how little snakes would run down an old snake's throat when in danger. We cut the old snake open and found twenty-four snakes inside. Several of them, each with a button on the tail, were fully developed and took right off when liberated. There were others coiled up like a snail, still in the process of developing, or hatching. I can't remember whether there were twenty-four that tried to crawl away or twenty-four altogether. Maybe Sid Smith can remember that feature."

As Walter Manley of Cotulla, Texas, told me his story, about 1910, while he was yet a boy, he was following a plow driven by a man named Ed Hall in a field in La Salle County, Texas, when the plow went through a "nest" of rattlesnakes. Thereupon, the old one rattled, spread her head out on the ground, mouth open, and gave "a kind of hissing." About a dozen little ones scampered into her mouth and disappeared. Hall killed the old snake, then cut or beat her open. The little ones emerged, very much alive, and were killed.

The hand is quicker than the eye; a rattlesnake's strike is quicker than the hand. But, from all accounts, the adult rattler's motions in preparation for receiving her young are deliberate. People like Asa Jones and Walter Manley are extraordinarily deliberate in their recollections. Not being scientific psychologists, they may not doubt their own memories, but they certainly do not believe that they have deceived themselves. No witness could be more positive than Jim C. Harris of Dallas, who has been incensed by scientific denials of what he considers absolute certainty. A part of his letter follows.

"It was in 1902 in a Kaffir corn field about the center of Wheeler Co., Texas. I and my cousin were plowing the maize with single plows, each plowing with a mule, side by side, and were talking as we plowed. The maize was just starting to head, about waist high. The harness was chain, and as it dragged against the maize it made quite a bit of noise. Suddenly I heard a rattler in the next middle to mine. I stopped my mule and looked over in the middle and saw a small rattler there, about even with the mule's head. She was holding her mouth open and was rattling at the same time. She was stretched out full length with tail towards me.

"While I was watching her and wondering why she was not trying to get away, I saw a small rattler run from the row of maize opposite her and it went straight to her mouth and crawled in of its own will and in perfect order. Then a second little rattler came in as did the first, then a third one, all coming in perfect order and of their own will and accord. No one, scientist or not, could make me believe that this thing I saw was a cannibalistic snake eating her young to satisfy her appetite. No man posing as a scientist can tell me not to believe what I saw with my own eyes while I was perfectly sober and in a normal condition mentally."

The next piece of testimony is from E. B. Ritchie, lawyer, of Mineral Wells, Texas. "Our Palo Pinto County ranch," he writes, "is in limestone formation, and back under the low shelving limestone ledges is where rattlesnakes like to den up. Some years ago our ranch foreman and I were passing in front of one of these ledges when we came upon a grown rattlesnake and several little ones that had presumably just crawled out from the shelter. The mother snake must have given some sound of alarm, though we heard nothing but the customary rattle; at any rate, upon our approach the little ones proceeded to take refuge inside the old snake, through her open mouth. We killed her, cut her open, and there the little ones were. The number, I do not remember.

"Incidentally, this ranch foreman, who is something of an amateur naturalist, corroborates the claim that rattlesnakes usually strike first and kill their prey before swallowing. He tells me that more than once he has seen a rattler lie in wait in weeds or other cover at the edge of a narrow trail and then at the approach of some small rodent strike it, waiting for it to die before beginning to swallow it."

John F. Houx, dealer in Texas volcanic pumicite, wrote

me from 1229 West Drew Avenue, Houston. Born in Missouri in 1855, he came to Texas with his parents in 1857 and settled with them on a farm in Grimes County. Now for his narrative:

"When I was about ten years old, I was chopping weeds in my father's watermelon patch. As I cut down a jimson-weed, I heard a hissing sound come from under it. I pulled the weed aside with my hoe and saw what I took to be a ground rattlesnake about two feet long. It kept hissing with mouth wide open. Right in front of it were about a dozen little snakes three or four inches long. They all wiggled into the mouth of the big snake. It closed its mouth and tried to get away. I hit it with my hoe and stunned it. Then I cut it in two, and the little snakes ran out on the ground around and under the old snake. I killed them with my hoe."

Another eyewitness account, from W. S. Edwards, 530 Alamito Avenue, Los Angeles, California, reads as follows:

"In 1919 I was living on a farm in Live Oak County, Texas, about eight miles from Oakville. One evening a little before sundown my Mexican and I hooked up a pair of mules to a buggy and started out to shoot some quail. A few hundred yards from the house I saw a rattlesnake in the grass beside the road. The Mexican was driving, and I told him to stop. I was about to shoot the snake when I noticed that her mouth was open and that little snakes were running into it. I watched until they all seemed to be in. Then the big snake closed her mouth and started to crawl away.

"I shot her head off, got out, picked up a stick and began squeezing the snake's body so that the little ones would be forced out. I squeezed out twenty-two little rattlesnakes. I never have claimed that she swallowed her young, but I do claim that she had a pocket below her stomach into which the little ones crawled, through her mouth. This is something definite that you can pass on to the scientific teachers."

My next testimonial is from F. M. Bradley, Eldorado, Texas. "About twenty years ago," he says, "I was heading some milo maize east of Eldorado. There was a big encino (live oak) growing in the field, and I stopped under it to unsaddle my horse. I had just pulled the saddle off and piled it down against the tree trunk when I discovered a rather large rattler lying nearby. I am sure it was a female. She gave a noticeably short buzz or two and then opened her mouth to the widest possible extent. Thereupon, little snakes, about four to six inches long, began to gather from all sides and to slither into the large snake's mouth. I killed her and then checked on what I thought I had seen. I found small snakes inside the old one. I don't recall how many there were, but when I got through with them there weren't any. In going after rattlesnakes I have always made it a rule not to leave any for seed."

The popular belief that snakes swallow their young for protective purposes was brought to the New World — the New World of rattlesnakes — by English colonists. I have never made any particular search for evidence of the phenomenon among North American Indians, but cannot recall having met in tomes of their lore any allusion to it. Raymond L. Ditmars says, in *Snakes of the World*, that "natives of the tropical American countries appear to know nothing about it."

Evincing in 1768 and again in 1776 a critical attitude towards the report of "intelligent folks" claiming to have seen "the viper open her mouth and admit her helpless young down her throat on sudden surprises," Gilbert White must have been among the earliest naturalists to question the belief. Still, he considered "candor and openness the very life of natural history," and this is one of the qualities of his nature that make *The Natural History of Selborne* as sweet and fresh in the twentieth century as it was in the eighteenth.

In Gilbert White's time (1720-1793), it was commonly believed that swallows hibernate in the ground like tortoises; all his life he was searching for evidence of both the hibernation and migration theories. Absolute proof of migration long since, of course, utterly disproved the theory of hibernation. Proof against the snake-swallowing theory is not so easy.

It is now a scientific truism that rattlesnakes are ovoviviparous — that the female not only generates eggs but hatches them inside herself, bringing forth the young fully formed, with a button on the tail and fangs in the mouth. Some snakes lay their eggs — are oviparous. It is also a scientific truism that, in the words of Raymond L. Ditmars, "Snakes never travel around with their young trailing after them like a string of ducks." As a general rule, apparently, the mother snake, whether ovoviviparous or oviparous, has no more concern for the young than a tick or a fly has for its hatched-out young.

Before he died at the age of sixty-six in 1942, Ditmars had come to be regarded by many as the most learned herpetologist the world has produced. From childhood his passion had been reptiles. It could not be charged that he knew snakes only in captivity. He had roamed the world hunting and studying reptilian life in its native habitats. Persistent stories of how various kinds of snakes, including rattlesnakes, swallow their young in order to protect them from danger made him search for evidence. Towards the end of his life he wrote:

"During thirty years of observation of serpents under all sorts of conditions in which they are found, I have watched them in areas in the temperate zones, on deserts and in the tropics, and have carried the story in mind. Thus the author has had every opportunity to verify the occurrence. I have never noted any hint of it.

"Hundreds of letters insisting upon this feat have come to my attention. These follow briefly expressed doubt in articles or remarks during lectures. The farmers of the

Middle West were particularly disturbed about an article intimating doubt of the story. . . . An avalanche of protest [made it] necessary to write a second article, backing my doubt with detailed explanation. This was followed by additional letters with details from observers who said they had actually seen the thing happen. . . .

"I have never heard a snake hiss as a call or signal to another. . . . It is doubtful if a litter of young snakes could be swallowed by an adult serpent and endure the salivary secretions of the mouth, which are of a glairy nature and would veneer and close their small nostrils. It would seem that they would thus be quickly smothered."

The most active herpetologist that Texas can claim was John K. Strecker, curator of the Baylor University Museum from 1903 until his death in 1933. He was eminently a field naturalist — so much so that the Ph.D.-ed laboratory biologists who make reputations by counting fruit flies regarded him as an outlander. He began publishing herpetological notes, based on field trips, in 1902 and publications of them continued into 1935, two years after his death. More than once he recurred to what he regarded as the "myth" of the snake swallowing its young. The point is that John K. Strecker was an out-of-doors observer. If he came to Austin for a meeting of the Texas Folklore Society, he spent most of the time in the hills or on the Colorado River looking for snakes, birds, snails or some other faunal form.

Many years ago a man named Tegetmier in England

offered a reward for "reasonable proof" that the female viper opens her mouth and allows her young to seek safety within her own body. The reward has never been claimed. In England, as in America, many eyewitness accounts have been published, and the British scientists, once hopeful for satisfying proof, have grown more and more skeptical. One of them, T. H. Gillespie, director of the Zoological Park, Edinburgh, after reviewing popular beliefs and reptilian physiology, concluded, "I should require very convincing evidence of fact before I could believe such a thing as a snake refuging her young in her throat ever happened."

So much has been published on the subject that the present treatise may well seem redundant. I have brought together a cloud of Texas witnesses. If some of them did not speak so unfalteringly about the "hissing" and "whistling" of rattlesnakes and did not make the little snakes so multitudinous, I should be perhaps more than almost persuaded. I have never heard a rattlesnake make any kind of noise except with the rattles. I have heard men who had spent their lives in a panther country assert that, because they had never heard its scream, that animal does not scream; yet panthers do scream sometimes. Ditmars says that the diamondback rattlesnake has "from eight to twelve young in a litter." A treatise based on scientific observation of thousands of Texas snakes, both in their native habitat and in the Reptile Garden connected with the Witte Museum at San Antonio, says of the Western diamond-

back rattlesnake and the Texas diamondback rattlesnake:
"A litter often numbers as high as thirty-five or forty.
Average, eleven to fifteen."

The dispositions of snakes, like the dispositions of men,
horses and other animals, certainly vary, the variations becoming more marked in the higher orders of species. Han-
dlers of thousands of rattlers in the San Antonio Reptile
Garden found that about one rattler in a hundred is mild
and docile, a "pet." Soon after one large diamond rattler
from Florida had given birth to nine young, Ditmars saw
her act in an aggressive manner that could be interpreted
only as a manifestation of the protective instinct. Yet every
snake is dependent upon itself for food as soon as it is
born. Nobody, insofar as I know, has ever claimed to have
seen an adult snake feeding its young. Basic biological
functions do not, cannot, vary in a species as individual
dispositions vary.

Is the Bite of a Rattlesnake
Fatal to Itself?

IT IS COMMONLY BELIEVED that an enraged rattlesnake is likely to bite itself and then quickly die of the poison injected into its system. At one meeting of the Texas Academy of Science in Waco, Dr. David Pettus, then of the University of Texas, later in the Zoology Department of Colorado A. and M. College, at Fort Collins, read a paper on the subject of self-poisoning by rattlesnakes. In it he said that stories of rattlesnakes biting themselves in order to keep from being taken alive are "misrepresentations." Laboratory experiments prove, he said, that it takes four doses of venom to kill a sidewinder and five doses to kill a diamondback. Unless a bite happened to be in a vital organ, it would hardly be fatal.

Mr. L. F. Chatfield of Harlingen, Texas, read a newspaper report on this scientific paper, waited six months to see a fellow witness, and then after corroboration by this witness wrote me as follows:

"In 1906 my wife's brother, C. E. Pye, now of Ben Bolt, Texas, and I were getting a wagonload of mesquite wood on the Burnet ranch in Knox County when we saw a rattle-snake about four feet long. We began teasing it with a limb. Suddenly, after striking at the limb a few times, it sank its fangs in its own body about six inches from the end of its tail. In a few moments it uncoiled and was dead — and I do mean dead — no waiting till sundown for that snake to die. After we cut and loaded our wood we looked at the snake again and it had not moved."

I sent a copy of this letter to Dr. David Pettus. Here is his reply: "I see several possible explanations for the snake's death. First, the teasing with the mesquite limb may have been too vigorous. The teasers may have broken the snake's back. This reminds me of a story told by Dave Alderson, who lives on the Gaines ranch just west of Austin. He said he had always heard that human spit is just as poisonous to a snake as its 'spit' is to human beings. One day while he and several other men were working in a rice field they found a cottonmouth moccasin and he decided to test the spit theory. After a mighty tussle with sticks and hoes they got the moccasin pinned down and its mouth pried open so that Dave could spit in it without danger of its spitting back. Well, sir, when they let that snake loose, it just crawled off a few feet and died all over. I wonder in just how many places they broke that snake's back in getting it pinned down.

"To get back to the rattlesnake that Mr. Chatfield teased with a mesquite limb, it could be that it was already in its death throes when found. Rattlesnakes are subject to certain enteric (intestinal) diseases, and often when they are on the verge of death from such they thrash about convulsively and accidentally bite themselves.

"Yet it is possible that the snake did die from the effect of venom injected into its own body. This is not in line with my research findings, but there is always the possibility of special circumstances, such as the venom's being deposited directly into a large blood vessel."

William G. McMillan, writing in that excellent magazine *Texas Game and Fish*, has this explanation: "A rattlesnake is not affected by a self-inflicted bite except where the long sharp fangs actually penetrate the reptile's vital organs. It is common practice for the snake to bite violently at the area where bodily pain has been inflicted. The resultant death is most likely due to the attacker's efforts rather than to the snake's own venom. Several species of nonpoisonous constrictor snakes, such as the king snake, are unaffected by bites received in combat with venomous snakes. They can and do suffer, however, when a poisonous snake's fangs penetrate vital organs."

In stories that have come to me about the rattlesnake's fanging itself to death, the evidence is usually pretty loose. Years ago Thomas A. Edwards of Lake Charles, Louisiana, supplied this instance. "One day while I was riding in the Dunn pasture in Live Oak County, Texas, looking for stray cattle, I came out of brush into an opening on which I saw a large rattlesnake making for cover. I got down and began chunking the snake (presumably with sticks). He fought like a mad tiger and rolled at me like a hoop, leaping eight or nine feet toward me, striking at the same time. I finally broke his back with a hit, which disabled him. In his rage he bit himself about three times and died."

When a witness tells me that he saw a rattlesnake make a hoop of himself and roll to the attack, I have to doubt.

Fred Haass, an Arizona trapper, gave me this account. While he was making camp near a rat den, he heard a rattlesnake, which no doubt had been trying to waylay a rat. Haass set fire to the den, made of dry sticks and cactus, and within a short time the rattler crawled out. He got a stick and tried to push the rattler into the fire. He did not injure it with the stick, he was sure, but the snake struck at it and hit himself, cutting a gash in its own body. At once it began writhing as if in extreme pain. Within three minutes it was stone dead. Haass was positive that the snake had not been burned.

Maybe not, but rattlesnakes are so sensitive to heat that one exposed for fifteen minutes to the direct rays of the sun at a temperature of one hundred degrees or even less will die.

The Mockingbird and the Rattlesnake

Roy BEDICHEK, late of the University of Texas, probably knew more about mockingbirds than any other man in the world. I owe to him the following account of the belligerent mockingbird's attack on a rattlesnake as written in a letter by Professor M. L. Williams of Southwestern University at Georgetown.

"In the summer of 1893 I was with my father on the Hinton ranch in McCulloch County, about ten miles west of Lohn Post Office. It was my job, or rather one of my jobs, to ride the fence around the pasture to see that no one had taken it down or that no cattle had gone out of the pasture.

"One day while on my job, I was nearing a dry branch on the west side of the pasture when I heard the sound of a rattler ahead. Riding cautiously, I was about thirty yards from the branch when I saw a large diamond rattler on the opposite bank, up under some bushes. The bushes were of the oak type, with no low underbrush, about twelve or more feet high. I could see the rattler clearly, his tail up, singing steadily. I knew there was something wrong, but I could see no cause for his anger. I decided to wait. After some minutes he suddenly stopped, and quickly started to run to the south. He was hardly well extended before a mockingbird darted from above and, flying down his length, struck at his head, circled above and quickly came down again. Sweeping down the snake's back each time, the bird made some four or five strikes at the head of the snake. Then the rattler stopped, coiled and struck several times, and began to rattle. I was fascinated, and rode up to within some twenty feet of the snake.

"Then I saw that one of his eyes was out and bleeding. My remembrance is that it was the right eye. In a few minutes the rattler made another dash, the mockingbird in the meantime having perched on a limb just above him. Immediately the bird went into action, as before. The snake again stopped. This fight went on for thirty minutes or more, the scene of action moving some thirty feet. The snake seemed afraid and to be trying to escape. The bird gave him no chance. Finally, the bird struck the other eye, held on and flapped vigorously, then darted up. The blood spurted from the eye. The rattler coiled and began striking in all directions, then sank his fangs into his own body, began rolling over, and finally came tumbling down the bank into the rocky branch, where he writhed in pain. The mockingbird flew up into the bushes and began to sing. I put the rattler out of his misery with a large stone.

The snake, of the large diamond type, was, I guess, about five feet long. I have seen other interesting contests between snakes, spiders, etc., but I think none more thrilling than this one."

Another account of the mockingbird-rattlesnake feud was given me in manuscript form by my good old friend, now dead, Don Alberto Guajardo of Piedras Negras, in Coahuila, Mexico. He had spent a long life in the vast ranch country of northern Mexico. Here is his account:

"One day while I was in the pasture with a shepherd boy, he said, 'There goes a large rattlesnake. Do you wish to kill it?'

" 'Surely,' I said, 'but where is it?'

" 'There, near that evergreen oak. It is going towards the brush.'

"My little daughter Josephine, at that time six or eight years old, was playing near, and I wanted her to have the opportunity to see the snake. I took a horsewhip and, guided by the shepherd boy, we followed to the spot where the snake was.

" 'Look, Master,' he pointed. 'Those birds you see have been driving the snake, to chase it away from their nest and the young.'

"A pair of mockingbirds were chattering loudly and darting around the snake, which was crawling slowly, dodging their intended pecks. The birds had their neck feathers ruffled in anger. They paid no attention to us as they continued to chase the snake. The boy wanted to kill the snake with the whip, but I said, 'Let us see what the mockingbirds are going to do.'

" 'They only chase it from their nest,' he said, 'but if there are two or three nests, all the old birds get together and kill the snake.'

"Then the shepherd struck the snake two or three times on the head. It became a little dizzy, and we withdrew somewhat to see what the birds would do. They flew down and pecked until they had pierced its head and killed it.

" 'Come on this side, Master,' said the shepherd boy. 'Yonder in' that evergreen oak, about eighty paces from here, is the nest from which the mockingbirds chased the snake.' We went directly to it. There on the ground beneath was the reptile's track. The boy then explained that many times he had killed snakes betrayed by the loud chattering of the mockingbirds."

It is too bad that Don Alberto allowed the shepherd boy to wound the snake and thus intercept the course of nature. He may have been mistaken in saying that the mockingbirds pierced the head of the snake instead of its eyes. The snake has no eyelids. I have seen several mockingbirds darting at a coachwhip snake and making a great deal of noise, but did not see the birds strike. Perhaps this was because the coachwhip was in a tree and the birds could not get a clear strike at it. They were certainly deterring it, however, from making progress towards a nest. One recalls Audubon's famous picture of a mockingbird picking out the eye of a rattlesnake actually in a nest in a tree.

The Eagle and the Serpent That Rattles

IT IS WELL KNOWN that eagles and hawks kill snakes, including rattlesnakes, for food. Yet few, indeed, of the multitudinous numbers of people who have seen many rattlesnakes and many hawks and eagles have ever seen the two species in juxtaposition. The phenomenon for most of us remains as remote as the legend, based upon natural history, behind the eagle and the serpent designed upon the Mexican flag. I have two accounts, which I believe to be authentic, of the struggle between eagle and rattler.

The first is from a rare book entitled *Adventures with Indians and Game* written by a man of considerable scientific knowledge named William A. Allen. Why any man, scientific or not scientific, should speak of a rattlesnake as "hissing" is beyond my understanding. Most people use a considerable number of words without any conception of precise meaning, and for such, snakes "hiss" in the same way that all females dressed in swimming suits are tagged as "bathing beauties." Anyway, here is Allen's description of the extraordinary episode he saw in the region of the Big Horn Mountains about 1877.

"On a beautiful September morning, as I was cantering along a mountain divide, drinking in the fresh air and admiring the beauty of mountain, river and forest spread out below me, the stillness was suddenly broken by the shrill scream of an eagle. High in the heavens I saw him, preparing to descend. Down, down he came, with the swiftness of a shooting star, until he had nearly touched the earth, when he spread his powerful pinions, slackened his speed, and with a sudden swoop, alighted on a great prairie rattler, about five feet long. A battle such as I had never before witnessed began.

"I rode slowly toward the combatants, getting as near as I could without disturbing them, and eagerly watched the progress of the fight. The bird was one of the largest of bald eagles (*Haliaeetus leucocephalus*), and the snake was a monster of its kind, fully three inches in diameter. The eagle, with its crest thrown backward, ran up to the snake and, with his wings, gave it a blow over the head which completely stunned it, just as it was in the act of striking at him with all its force. Quick as thought, the eagle then caught the snake in his talons, soared about ten feet in the air, gave it a furious shaking and let it fall to earth, where it lay coiled in a warlike attitude, rattling and hissing.

"The eagle made a second attack in the same manner, but the snake watched its chance, and, when the eagle was close enough, thrust its head between the bird's head and wing, and, with a desperate effort, wound itself around the

[185]

eagle's body. It looked for a moment as though the power-ful bird must die. But, with a violent flap of his wings, he broke the deadly embrace, caught the snake, gave it a number of jerks, and threw it down again. The blood was oozing from several places in the rattler's body and this seemed to make the eagle more excited than ever.

"The antagonists now remained some feet apart and seemed to be resting, though the rattler kept up a deep buzzing. . . . The eagle next tried another plan, wheeling around his enemy in a circle, but the serpent managed al-ways to face him. Thus foiled, the eagle began to whip the rattler with the tips of his wings, his head well thrown back, but the snake dodged the blows. The eagle then made a feint, jumped to one side and struck the snake a fearful blow; caught it up by the middle and shook it until the snake was about to twine itself around his body, when he again threw it to the ground. Both then showed signs of great fatigue, but neither seemed inclined to give way.

"The eagle ran round and round his victim, but still the snake managed to hold him off, until he threw back his head and made a desperate drive. The snake then struck with all of its force as the wing of the eagle came in contact with its head, and, while trying to coil again around the eagle's body, was caught and carried into the air, where it was almost jerked in twain. When it reached the ground its entrails were hanging out, and it writhed and twisted in great pain. The proud bird stood looking on with the victorious air of a pugilist who has won a world-renowned battle.

"For the first time he cast his large eyes upon me, showing neither surprise nor anger at my presence. He seemed to understand that I would not molest him, for he turned to the snake and gave it another good shaking, to make sure of its death. . . . When the agonies of death were over and his enemy had ceased writhing, he stretched his wings, seized his prey where the skin was not broken, and, with a steady flight, bore it to the highest crag of the neighboring mountain. As he slowly winged his way, the huge serpent was visible hanging from his powerful claws. The fight had lasted about three-quarters of an hour. Had the eagle been less careful of his head, he could have torn the snake to atoms in a moment, but he seemed to realize the poisonous nature of the snake, and gained his victory by the exercise of his strategic instinct."

The second account is from another privately published book, *Thirty Years on the Frontier* by Robert McReynolds. Sometime in the 1880's, as he tells, he and a man named Mark Witherspoon were in the Palm Desert of California.

"How it began," McReynolds wrote, "I did not see. I was standing near the top of a big stony crag that glistened in the bright light, looking over the vast opens and great basins of the Palm Desert which we were to cross, when my attention was attracted by the flop of something striking the sands a hundred feet away. I could not see what it was, but a moment later I saw an eagle swoop down and rise slowly, holding within its mailed claws a snake. The big bird soared up a hundred feet or more and shook the snake loose, which fell twisting and coiling with a distinctly audible flop — the noise that first attracted my attention. Again and again the bird swooped, arose with the serpent and dropped it, while Witherspoon drew closer and closer to watch.

"The eagle — a young one, as we could tell by its size and plumage — struck and failed to rise. Witherspoon was now close enough to see everything that happened.

"The young bird had almost exhausted itself in its struggles with the snake, and may, too, have been bitten. At any rate, it was upon the sands, its wings slightly spread, as if from the heat — its mouth open. The snake was recovering from its jolting fall, and slowly gathering its coils.

"It rested a moment in position, and then struck the eagle, the fangs entering the corner of the bird's mouth, in the soft tissues at the base of the beak.

"The eagle recovered from the shock, stood motionless a few seconds, while the rattler watched as only a rattler can, and, spreading out its wings, toppled over.

"Then the man put forth his hand. There was a puff of white smoke in the clear air and the report of a pistol rang among the glistening wind-polished rocks, and the snake was a mangled, bright, still thing that the ants began to gather about."

It is maudlin, unintelligent and hypocritical for man, the most predatory of all animals, to be always taking sides in the natural conflicts between other animals. Probably the snake would have crawled away to die anyway, had the fellow not shot it.

Wild Gobbler and Rattlesnake Fight

THE BIRD'S HOSTILITY TO RATTLESNAKES is generally known, but for the most part only in a general way. All birds are by nature opposed to all snakes. W. P. Hubbard wrote to me from California the description of a fight between a big rattlesnake and a big wild gobbler that he watched in the Kit Carson National Forest, of northern New Mexico, some years ago. I know Mr. Hubbard only through correspondence, but that has been rather extensive and, without reserve, I accept as fact every detail of his account. It follows without quotation marks.

One mid-morning in June I rode out of a canyon that opened into a meadow, tied my horse in the shade of a spruce tree, and walked to a spring at the base of a low bluff. After drinking, I climbed up on a flat-topped boulder shaded by aspens and stretched out to rest and to look. About twenty feet below me the spring water disappeared into bare sandy soil. Except for that bare patch of ground, the meadow was heavily grassed. It was irregularly fringed all around with forest trees.

I hadn't been resting long when a sharp "Obble, obble, obble" cut the thin still air. Moments later I spotted a big gobbler, followed by three hens, emerging from the woods across the meadow. No wind was stirring, but presently I noticed that the tall thick grass about the four wild turkeys was alive with movement. I deduced that it must be caused by poults, and soon a little fellow jumping high for an insect exposed himself. Others leaped into view also. From the swayings in the grass, I estimated that there were between thirty and forty of the young turkeys, probably about six weeks old.

The flock fed slowly towards the spring. The gobbler was a giant. Now and then he made a running leap, his wings half opening, as he dashed after a grasshopper. One of the older birds was always in alert watchfulness while the others fed. When they were about halfway across the meadow, they changed their course and drifted towards the mouth of the canyon. If they had caught sight of my saddled horse, they would instantly have left, but they veered back towards the spring. Upon approaching the point of a jut of timber to my right, they all stopped at a commanding "Putt-putt-putt" from the gobbler. They were near enough now that the deep purple heads of the adult birds and the sheen on their bluish, black-brown bodies were brilliant in the sunshine against the yellow of the meadow. The gobbler said "Purt-purt," and instantly tufts of grass stirred as the flock continued their advance.

Several poults emerged into full view. One hopped up

on a fallen tree, spread its immature wings, and ran down the trunk. The tree had been there a long time and lay flat on the ground. When the poult was about a foot from its point, I saw the form of a yellowish-brown rattlesnake shoot upward from short grass at the edge of the tree trunk and knock the poult to the ground.

Its terrified cry brought the gobbler, gobbling sharply, to the clear ground, while the hens, with alarmed purts, and their coveys hastily moved back into tall grass. The young ones froze in the covering and the old hens, with a roaring of wings, zoomed upward and across the meadow to glide down into spruces.

The gobbler reached the poult just as it ceased to cry and fluttered its last flutter. Meanwhile the rattler was crawling out of the grass into full view on the grassless ground. The two confronted each other maybe forty-five feet, not over fifty feet, from the boulder on which I watched, unobserved, looking down. The gobbler arched his wings, leaped, and landed, feathers ruffled in defiance, facing the rattler five or six feet away. The rattler coiled, buzzing angrily. The dead poult was midway between them.

Presently the gobbler raised one foot and took a cautious step forward. As he started to take another step, the weaving rattler struck. At the same time, and just as swiftly it seemed, the gobbler shot upward, so thrashing the air with his great wings that a film of dust rose from the ground beneath him. He had his legs pulled back so that his spurs could dig into the rattler. He came down beyond striking distance. I can't tell how he did it, but he was hammering with his beak at the rattler's head while he was coming down out of reach of the fangs.

The rattler moved forward and coiled beside the poult's body. The gobbler began to circle with short, quick steps, forward and backward, closing up the distance between him and the rattler, which was all the time buzzing and turning itself to face the attacker. Again it struck, missed, struck again, hitting the gobbler's beard a glancing blow that caused it to fly sideways. I could not see the hit, but I saw plainly the effect of the impact on the beard. At every strike, the gobbler's spurs came as close to the rattler as the rattler's fangs came to him.

Part of the rattler's body was now over the poult. At a sudden move by the gobbler, the rattler struck again, missed, and was knocked out of coil by one of the turkey's wings. Before it could straighten out, the gobbler either flipped with his beak or kicked (I could not tell which) the poult a good six feet away. When the dust settled, the rattler was recoiled, weaving its head from side to side, buzzing in frenzied rage. But now its strikes did not seem so swift. At another advance by the circling gobbler, it hit close enough to get a feather in its open mouth. I saw the feather as the rattler drew its head back.

Without giving the snake time to recoil, the gobbler spurred it a few inches behind the head, tearing a gash in its side. It left a thin trail of blood on the sand as it drew slowly back to a half coil, then revived sufficiently to complete the coil. Twice again it struck, with diminished vigor, at the unflagging gobbler.

Suddenly the gobbler stopped circling, cupped his wings, and stood waiting. The rattler curved a part of its body into a U and made two or three short, feeble strikes. Now the gobbler leaped and came down, hooking a spur into the snake at the base of the head. At the impact the snake's body straightened out, and the gobbler was instantly pecking his powerful beak into the back with the rapidity of a trip-hammer.

Its head still hooked on the curved spur, the snake's body began to thrash about. With a startled "Obble, obble," the gobbler leaped up, kicking to release the snake. For a few seconds the air was full of flying legs, feet, feathers and snake, while the rattles still buzzed and the gobbler still gobbled. The gobbler's spur came free. The snake was dead, and with nervous putts the victor backed off and stood eyeing his conquered enemy.

Soon he fanned out his tail, spread his wings into a full strut, and gobbled forth a throaty cry of victory. He strutted up to the dead snake, beaked it a few times, and kicked it. Then he strutted to the dead poult. While he stood there, a hen gave an inquiring gobble. He responded, and soon the three hens appeared out of the spruces. They sailed over the meadow and hit the ground near their lord. While they looked on, he strutted around and over the dead rattler. They did not get near it, but moved back into the grass, where one of them putted the poults out of cover. The hens now led the young towards timber, the gobbler following with an air of deliberate independence.

When the turkeys had disappeared, I examined the rattlesnake. It had a gash an inch and a half long on its side, ten inches back from the head. The gobbler's spur, entering at the base of the head, had punctured the spinal column and come out through the top of the snake's skull. There were five punctures from the gobbler's beak in the skull and eleven punctures along the back, a number of them made after the snake was dead. I skinned out the rattler, had the hide tanned, and still have it. It is four feet, four and one-half inches long and is attached to eight rattles and a button.

The battle lasted about half an hour. I did not think to keep accurate count of the number of times the rattler struck, but it was not less than a dozen times.

The Rattlesnake-Guarded Treasure

IF I LIVED TO BE as old as Methuselah, I'd never forget Longworth. He was tall and lank and deliberate, his black eyes and soft voice full of memories and dreams. Until the day of his death there was not a gray streak in his black hair, thick and heavy like an Indian's. He wore a long black mustache that drooped like the ends of a pair of horns on a Texas steer.

I first met him in San Antonio, where so many stories and storybook characters are always waiting. He had been working, off and on for years, with financial backing from a San Antonio lawyer, on cleaning out "an old tunnel" in one of the hills of the San Saba River country. He was sure that some day he would reach two thousand bars of silver placed there by the Spaniards — product of the fabulous San Saba (Lost Bowie) Mine. He had what he called "the radio sleuth" — an instrument designed to locate buried treasure. He told me many stories — this is one of them.

An old one-armed sheepherder by the name of Pedro Hernandez used to live out in the Uvalde country. He was a good shot and used to carry a brass-bellied .44 Winchester with him, using the stub of his arm to support the barrel when he aimed at anything. One evening while he was up on a knoll watching his sheep graze down a deep draw, he noticed the leaders of the flock suddenly wheel and start up the draw. He knew they had scented danger. Not far below the place where they had turned, a second draw emptied into the main one. At the point of the junction, hunched down close to a cliff, Pedro's good eyes made out a coyote. He fired.

When the smoke cleared away — for he used old-time black powder — he could not make out any coyote, dead or alive. He was sure he had hit the animal; the bottom land was so open that not even a jackrabbit could hide there. Puzzled as to how the coyote had disappeared, he walked down to investigate. In the rocky cliff at which he had seen the coyote, but out of view from the knoll from which he had shot, Pedro found the answer to his puzzle. There was a cave running back under a shelf, and coyote tracks led into it. The cave went back too far for a man's eyes to pierce the darkness. Pedro had made no noise. He knew that if he remained silent, the coyote would, if not dead, soon come out. He took a position whence he could watch the opening and waited. Sure enough, before long, the coyote's head appeared. Pedro downed him in his track this time. Then he scalped him, for there was a bounty on coyotes. It was summertime and the pelt was worthless.

Many times Pedro had passed up and down these draws, but he had never before noticed the cave. He had plenty of matches. He gathered some dried sotol leaves for torches and went inside to look around. The mouth was narrow and well concealed by a rock formation and a bush, but the farther back the old sheepherder went the bigger he found the opening. Finally, lighting matches and burning the sotol leaves, he made out a pile of something on the level floor in the middle of the cave. As he got close to it, it looked like a pile of dirt. It was so far back that by now he could just see a little point of light marking the mouth of the cave.

Right at the piled-up object, he could not make out what it was. He kicked it, and the kick broke open a kind of fiber sacking. Gold coins poured out on the dusty floor. The dust was as dry as dry lime. There were several sacks. They were made out of a kind of matting, the fiber long ago having lost all life. Pedro tried to pick up one of the sacks, but where he caught hold of it, it pulled apart and the gold money just tumbled out.

As anybody would do, Pedro now began to pick up coins to fill his pockets. He was operating mostly in the dark, for those sotol leaves will not burn much longer than a match. He pulled off his shirt and tied knots in the sleeves at the wrists, in order to use them as bags, but the shirt was old and the sleeves had so many holes in them that he was not making much headway in bagging the gold.

Then all at once he heard the buzzing of rattlesnakes. The buzzing sounded all around him. He dropped the shirt and the buzzing stopped. He lit matches and looked around, but not a snake was in sight. He picked up the shirt and made two steps toward the opening of the cave. The buzzing set up again. He retreated to the pile of gold — so that he could stand on top of it and be clear of the snakes. He again dropped the shirt and the buzzing again hushed.

Pedro started for the opening. The buzzing of rattlesnakes became louder and shriller than ever. That sound will almost paralyze a man at times, even when he is looking at the snake making it in broad daylight, a safe distance off. But Pedro was not too paralyzed to jump back to the pile of gold. Instinctively he cast the coins from his pockets, every coin he had meant to carry off.

The den, the cave, became as silent as the darkness was deep. He lit a match, burned his last flare of sotol leaves. Not a snake, not even a snake's trail, lay on the dusty floor. When Pedro headed for the mouth of the cave this time, there was no opposition. In the sunlight at the entrance, once he was outside, he stopped and looked back. There, a few feet away, he could see his own tracks and the tracks of the coyote — but no snake tracks.

It was summertime, as has been said. Rattlesnakes do not den up in the summer, though during the day they keep in coolish places. At that time of year they do not come together in great numbers as when they hibernate in caves. Pedro knew this well. He knew he had seen a fortune in gold. He wondered if he had imagined the rattling. He had not, after all, seen even the sign of a snake. He had not smelled rattlesnakes — and their odor is as strong as that of javelina hogs when in excitement they cast musk from their musk bags.

Pedro wanted some of that gold. He gathered some more sotol leaves. He stepped around the point of the draw, looked up it, and saw that his dog was watching the sheep. Then he did what not one other Mexican sheepherder out of a thousand would have done. He went back into the cave. When he got to the sacks and began gathering his pockets full of the gold coins, he forgot all about rattlesnakes. Soon he had all he could carry and started briskly towards the pinpoint of light.

At the first step a sound of rattling went up that seemed to fill the cave. He stopped dead still, dropping what money he held clutched in his one hand. The rattling continued. He lit a match, and there in front of him the biggest rattler he had ever seen was reared up waist-high, ready to strike. It is hardly necessary to say that he backed up to the sacks, where he emptied the last coin out of his pockets. The rattling died down. He was too weak for a while to attempt walking. Finally he got his breath and the blood began to circulate in his body again. When he lit a match, he could not see a snake. He said he did not know whether he walked or crawled or ran out of the cave. Once out, he had to lie down and rest awhile before he could make it to where he heard the bells on his sheep.

Pedro Hernandez told Longworth that he believed the snakes were evil spirits guarding the money. If they had been real snakes, he said, they would have left trails on the powdered earth of the cave floor. There was not a sign where he had seen them, and not a smell.

"Did you ever go back in the cave again?" Longworth asked him.

"No, señor, and not for all the gold in the world would I go back."

"Will you make the sign of the cross, Pedro, and swear that you are telling me the truth about seeing the sacks of gold?"

And Pedro made the sign of the Holy Cross and solemnly said, "I tell only truth."

He told Longworth he would guide him to the mouth of the cave. Finally, Longworth started to the ranch from Uvalde, but his car burned out two bearings and he had to give up the trip. Some time after this a friend of his went to the ranch to get Pedro's guidance, but the rancher ran him off. This was during prohibition days, and Longworth later learned that a still was located on the draw not far from where the coyote led Pedro to discover the cave. No doubt the cave is still there, its darkness as withholding as when Pedro emerged from it for the last time.